BODY LANGUAGE

**How to read others' thoughts
by their gestures**

BODY LANGUAGE

How to read others' thoughts
by their gestures

Allan Pease

PEASE TRAINING INTERNATIONAL

© Allan Pease 1981, 1998
All rights reserved
No part of this publication may be reproduced or
transmitted, in any form or by any means, without the
prior permission of the publisher.
First published 1981 by
Pease Training International, Phone (02) 9979 9000, Fax (02) 9979 9099
P.O. Box 12, Mona Vale, NSW 2103, Australia
Website www.peasetraining.com
Published in USA as "Signals: How to Use Body Language
for Power, Success and Love".
110th Reprint
National Library of Australia
Cataloguing-in-Publication data

Pease, Allan
Body Language.
ISBN 0 9593658 0 X.

1. Nonverbal communication (Psychology). 2. Movement,
Psychology of. I. Title.
158'.2

Edited by Jacqueline Kent
Illustrated by John Hepworth
Printed by Australian Print Group
Maryborough, Vic.

Publishers and Distributors:
Australia: Harper-Collins Pty Ltd
New Zealand: Harper-Collins Pty Ltd
South East Asia: Reed International
South Africa: Oxford University Press
Europe: Sheldon Press
North America: Bantam Books
United Kingdom: Sheldon Press
Asia: Reed International
Translated into every major language.

Contents

Acknowledgments

I wish to thank the following people who have directly and indirectly contributed to this book: Noel Bishop, Raoul Boiele, Ty Boyd, Sue Brannigan, Matthew Braund, Doug Constable, John Cooke, Sharon Cooper, Chris Corck, Brett Davies, Dr. Andre Davril, George Deveraux, Rob Edmonds, Iven Frangi, Rex Gamble, Dave Goodwin, Jan Goodwin, Paul Gresham, Gerry Hatton, John Hepworth, Bob Heussler, Gay Huber, Professor Phillip Hunsaker, Dianne Joss, Jacqueline Kent, Ian McKillop, Delia Mills, Desmond Morris, Virginia Moss, Wayne Mugridge, John Nevin, Peter Opie, Diana O'Sullivan, Richard Otton, Ray Pease, David Plenderleith, David Rose, Richard Salisbury, Kim Sheumack, Jan Smith, Tom Stratton, Ron Tacchi, Steve Tokoly, Keith Weber, Alan White, Rob Winch and the Australian Jaycees.

Introduction

When I first heard about 'body language' at a seminar in 1971, I became so excited about it that I wanted to learn more. The speaker told us about some research done by Professor Ray Birdwhistell at the University of Louisville, which had shown that more human communication took place by the use of gestures, postures, position and distances than by any other method. At that time I had been a commission salesman for several years and had undergone many long, intensive courses on selling techniques, but none of these courses had ever mentioned anything about the non-verbal aspects or implications of face-to-face encounters.

My own investigations showed that little useful information was available on body language and, although libraries and universities had records of the studies done on it, most of this information consisted of closely set manuscripts and theoretical assumptions compiled in an objective manner by people who had little or no practical experience in dealing with other human beings. This does not mean that their work was not important; simply that most of it was too technical to have any practical application or use by a layman like myself.

In writing this book, I have summarized many of the studies by the leading behavioral scientists and have combined them with similar research done by people in other professions—sociology, anthropology, zoology, education, psychiatry, family counseling, professional negotiating and selling. The book also includes many 'how to' features developed from the countless reels of videotape and film made by myself and others, plus some of the experiences and encounters that I have had with the thousands of people that I have interviewed, recruited, trained, managed and sold to over the past fifteen years.

This book is by no means the last word on body language, nor does it contain any of the magic formulas promised by some of the books in the bookstores. Its purpose is to make the reader more aware of his own non-verbal cues and signals and to demonstrate how people communicate with each other using this medium.

This book isolates and examines each component of body language and gesture, though few gestures are made in isolation from others; I have at the same time tried to avoid oversimplifying. Non-verbal communication is, however, a complex process involving people, words, tone of voice and body movements.

˙There will always be those who throw up their hands in horror and claim that the study of body language is just another means by which scientific knowledge can be used to exploit or dominate others by reading their secrets or thoughts. This book seeks to give the reader greater insight into communication with his fellow humans, so that he may have a deeper understanding of other people and, therefore, of himself. Understanding how something works makes living with it easier, whereas a lack of understanding and ignorance promote fear and superstition and make us more critical of others. A birdwatcher does not study birds so that he can shoot them down and keep them as trophies. In the same way, the acquisition of knowledge and skills in non-verbal communication serves to make every encounter with another person an exciting experience.

This book was originally intended as a working manual for salespeople, sales managers and executives and, in the ten years that it has taken to research and compile, it has been expanded in such a way that any person, regardless of his or her vocation or position in life, can use it to obtain a better understanding of life's most complex event—a face-to-face encounter with another person.

ALLAN PEASE

One

A Framework for Understanding

As we approach the end of the twentieth century, we are witnessing the emergence of a new kind of social scientist— the non-verbalist. Just as the birdwatcher delights in watching birds and their behavior, so the non-verbalist delights in watching the non-verbal cues and signals of human beings. He watches them at social functions, at beaches, on television, at the office or anywhere that people interact. He is a student of behavior who wants to learn about the actions of his fellow humans so that he may ultimately learn more about himself and how he can improve his relationships with others.

It seems almost incredible that, over the million or more years of man's evolution, the non-verbal aspects of communication have been actively studied on any scale only since the 1960s and that the public has become aware of their existence only since Julius Fast published a book about body language in 1970. This was a summary of the work done by behavioral scientists on non-verbal communication up until that time, and even today, most people are still ignorant of the existence of body language, let alone its importance in their lives.

Charlie Chaplin and many other silent movie actors were the pioneers of non-verbal communication skills; they were the only means of communication available on the screen.

Each actor was classed as good or bad by the extent to which he could use gestures and other body signals to communicate effectively. When talking films became popular and less emphasis was placed on the non-verbal aspects of acting, many silent movie actors faded into obscurity and those with good verbal skills prevailed.

As far as the technical study of body language goes, perhaps the most influential pre-twentieth-century work was Charles Darwin's *The Expression of the Emotions in Man and Animals* published in 1872. This spawned the modern studies of facial expressions and body language and many of Darwin's ideas and observations have since been validated by modern researchers around the world. Since that time, researchers have noted and recorded almost one million non-verbal cues and signals. Albert Mehrabian found that the total impact of a message is about 7 percent verbal (words only) and 38 percent vocal (including tone of voice, inflection and other sounds) and 55 percent non-verbal. Professor Birdwhistell made some similar estimates of the amount of non-verbal communication that takes place among humans. He estimated that the average person actually speaks words for a total of about ten or eleven minutes a day and that the average sentence takes only about 2.5 seconds. Like Mehrabian, he found that the verbal component of a face-to-face conversation is less than 35 percent and that over 65 percent of communication is done non-verbally.

Most researchers generally agree that the verbal channel is used primarily for conveying information, while the non-verbal channel is used for negotiating interpersonal attitudes, and in some cases is used as a substitute for verbal messages. For example, a woman can give a man a look to kill'; she will convey a very clear message to him without opening her mouth.

Regardless of culture, words and movements occur together with such predictability that Birdwhistell says that a well-trained person should be able to tell what movement a man is making by listening to his voice. In like manner, Birdwhistell learned how to tell what language a person was speaking, simply by watching his gestures.

Many people find difficulty in accepting that humans are still biologically animals. *Homo sapiens* is a species of primate, a hairless ape that has learned to walk on two limbs and has a clever, advanced brain. Like any other species, we are dominated by biological rules that control our actions, reactions, body language and gestures. The fascinating thing is that the human animal is rarely aware of his postures, movements and gestures that can tell one story while his voice may be telling another.

Perceptiveness, Intuition and Hunches

From a technical point of view, whenever we call someone 'perceptive' or 'intuitive', we are referring to his or her ability to read another person's non-verbal cues and to compare these cues with verbal signals. In other words, when we say that we have a 'hunch' or 'gut feeling' that someone has told us a lie, we really mean that their body language and their spoken words do not agree. This is also what speakers call audience awareness, or relating to a group. For example, if the audience were sitting back in their seats with chins down and arms crossed on their chest, a 'perceptive' speaker would get a hunch or feeling that his delivery was not getting across. He would become aware that he needed to take a different approach to gain audience involvement. Likewise, a speaker who was not 'perceptive' would blunder on regardless.

Women are generally more perceptive than men, and this fact has given rise to what is commonly referred to as 'women's intuition'. Women have an innate ability to pick up and decipher non-verbal signals, as well as having an accurate eye for small details. This is why few husbands can lie to their wives and get away with it and why, conversely, most women can pull the wool over a man's eyes without his realizing it.

This female intuition is particularly evident in women who have brought up young children. For the first few years, the mother relies solely on the non-verbal channel to communicate with the child and this is believed to be the reason why women often become more perceptive negotiators than men.

Inborn, Genetic, Learned and Cultural Signals

Much research and debate has been done to discover whether non-verbal signals are inborn, learned, genetically transferred or acquired in some other way. Evidence was collected from observation of blind and/or deaf people who could not have learned non-verbal signals through the auditory or visual channels, from observing the gestural behavior of many different cultures around the world and from studying the behavior of our nearest anthropological relatives, the apes and monkeys.

The conclusions of this research indicate that some gestures fall into each category. For example, most primate children are born with the immediate ability to suck, indicating that this is either inborn or genetic. The German scientist Eibl-Eibesfeldt found that the smiling expressions of children born deaf and blind occur independently of learning or copying, which means that these must also be inborn gestures. Ekman, Friesen and Sorenson supported some of Darwin's original beliefs about inborn gestures when they studied the facial expressions of people from five widely different cultures. They found that each culture used the same basic facial gestures to show emotion, which led them to the conclusion that these gestures must be inborn.

When you cross your arms on your chest, do you cross left

over right or right over left? Most people cannot confidently describe which way they do this until they try it. Where one way feels comfortable, the other feels completely wrong. Evidence suggests that this may well be a genetic gesture that cannot be changed.

Debate still exists as to whether some gestures are culturally learned and become habitual, or are genetic. For example, most men put on a coat right arm first; most women put it on left arm first. When a man passes a woman in a crowded street, he usually turns his body towards her as he passes; she usually turns her body away from him. Does she instinctively do this to protect her breasts? Is this an inborn female reaction or has she learned to do this by unconsciously watching other females?

Much of our basic non-verbal behavior is learned and the meaning of many movements and gestures is culturally determined. Let us now look at these aspects of body language.

Some Basics and Their Origins

Most of the basic communication gestures are the same all over the world. When people are happy they smile; when they are sad or angry they frown or scowl. Nodding the head is almost universally used to indicate 'yes' or affirmation. It appears to be a form of head lowering and is probably an inborn gesture, as it is also used by deaf and blind people. Shaking the head from side to side to indicate 'no' or negation is also universal and may well be a gesture that is learned in infancy. When a baby has had enough milk, he turns his head from side to side to reject his mother's breast. When the young child has had enough to eat, he shakes his head from side to side to stop his parent's attempt to spoon feed him and in this way he quickly learns to use the head shaking gesture to show disagreement or a negative attitude.

The evolutionary origin of some gestures can be traced to our primitive animal past. Baring the teeth is derived from the act of attacking and is still used by modern man in the form of a sneer and other such hostile gestures, even though he will not attack with his teeth. Smiling was originally a threat gesture, but today it is done in conjunction with non-threatening gestures to show pleasure.

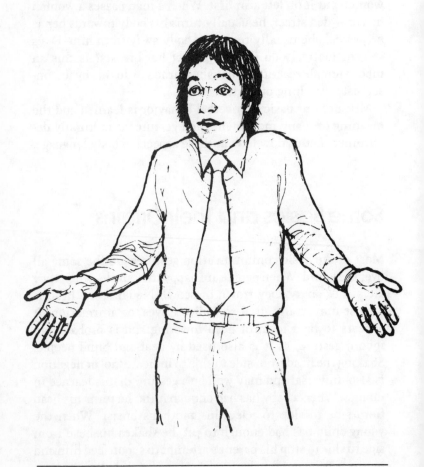

Figure 1   *The shoulder shrug gesture*

The shoulder shrug is also a good example of a universal gesture that is used to show that a person does not know or understand what you are talking about. It is a multiple gesture that has three main parts: exposed palms, hunched shoulders and raised brow.

Just as verbal language differs from culture to culture, so the non-verbal language may also differ. Whereas one gesture may be common in a particular culture and have a clear interpretation, it may be meaningless in another culture or even have a completely opposite meaning. Take, for example, the cultural interpretations and implications of three common hand gestures, the ring gesture, the thumb-up and V sign.

Figure 2   *'Everything's OK!'*

The Ring or 'OK' Gesture

This gesture was popularized in America during the early nineteenth century, apparently by the newspapers that, at the time, were starting a craze of using initials to shorten common phrases. There are many different views about what the initials 'OK' stand for, some believing it stood for 'all correct' which may have been misspelled as 'oll korrect', while others say that it means the opposite of 'knock-out', that is, K.O. Another popular theory is that it is an abbreviation of 'Old Kinderhook', from the birthplace of a nineteenth century American president who used the initials as a campaign slogan. Which theory is the correct one we may never know, but it seems that the ring itself represents the letter 'O' in the 'OK' signal. The 'OK' meaning is common to all English-speaking countries and, although its meaning is fast spreading across Europe and Asia, it has other origins and meanings in certain places. For example, in France it also means 'zero' or 'nothing'; in Japan it can mean 'money'; in some Mediterranean countries it is an orifice signal, often used to imply that a man is homosexual.

For overseas travelers, the safest rule to obey is, 'When in Rome, do as the Romans do'. This can help avoid possibly embarrassing circumstances.

The Thumb-Up Gesture

In the U.S., Britain, Australia and New Zealand the thumb-up gesture has three meanings; it is commonly used by hitch-hikers who are thumbing a ride, it is an OK signal, and when the thumb is jerked sharply upwards it becomes an insult signal, meaning 'up yours' or 'sit on this'. In some countries, such as Greece, its main meaning is 'get stuffed', so you can imagine the dilemma of the American hitchhiker using this gesture in that country! When Italians count from one to five, they use this gesture to mean 'one' and the index finger then becomes 'two', whereas most Americans and English people count 'one' on the index finger and two on the middle finger. In this case the thumb will represent the number 'five'.

Figure 3   *'No worries.'*

The thumb is also used, in combination with other gestures, as a power and superiority signal or in situations where people try to get us 'under their thumb'. A later chapter takes a closer look at the use of the thumb in these particular contexts.

The V Sign

This sign is popular throughout Great Britain and Australia, and carries an 'up yours' interpretation. Winston Churchill popularized the V for victory sign during World War II, but his two-fingered version was done with the palm facing out, whereas the palm faces towards the speaker for the obscene insult version. In most parts of Europe, however, the palm facing in version still means 'victory' so that an Englishman who uses it to tell a European to 'get stuffed' could leave the European wondering about what victory the Englishman meant. This signal also means the number two in many parts of Europe.

These examples show that cultural misinterpretations of gestures can produce embarrassing results and that a person's cultural background should always be considered before jumping to conclusions about his or her body language or gestures. Therefore, unless otherwise specified, our discussion should be considered culturally specific, that is, generally pertaining to adult, white middle-class people raised in North America, Great Britain, Australia and other places where English is the primary language.

Gesture Clusters

One of the most serious mistakes a novice in body language can make is to interpret a solitary gesture in isolation from other gestures or other circumstances. For example, scratching the head can mean a number of things—dandruff, fleas, sweating, uncertainty, forgetfulness or lying, depending on the other gestures that occur at the same time, so we must always look at gesture clusters for a correct reading.

Like any other language, body language consists of words, sentences and punctuation. Each gesture is like a single word and a word may have several different meanings. It is only when you put the word into a sentence with other words that you can fully understand its meaning. Gestures come in 'sentences' and invariably tell the truth about a person's feelings or attitudes. The 'perceptive' person is one who can read the non-verbal sentences and accurately match them against the person's verbal sentences.

Figure 4 shows a common critical evaluation gesture cluster. The main one is the hand-to-face gesture, with the index finger pointing up the cheek while another finger covers the mouth and the thumb supports the chin. Further evidence that this listener is critical of the speaker is seen by the fact that the legs are tightly crossed and the arm crosses the body (defensive) while the head and chin are down (hostility). This non-verbal 'sentence' says something like, 'I don't like what you are saying and I disagree with you.'

Congruence

If you, as the speaker, were to ask the listener shown in Figure 4 to give his opinion of what you have just said and he said that he disagreed with you, his non-verbal signals would be congruent with his verbal sentences, that is, they would match or be consistent. If, however, he said he was enjoying what you had to say, he would be lying because his words and gestures would be incongruent. Research shows that non-verbal signals carry about five times as much impact as the verbal channel and that, when the two are incongruent, people rely on the non-verbal message; the verbal content may be disregarded.

We often see a politician standing behind a lectern with his arms tightly folded across his chest (defensive) and chin down (critical or hostile), while telling his audience how receptive and open he is to the ideas of young people. He may attempt to convince the audience of his warm, humane approach while giving short, sharp karate chops to the lectern. Sigmund Freud once noted that while a patient was verbally expressing happiness with her marriage, she was unconsciously slipping her wedding ring on and off her finger. Freud was aware of the significance of this unconscious gesture and was not surprised when marriage problems began to surface.

Observation of gesture clusters and congruence of the verbal and non-verbal channels are the keys to accurate interpretation of body language.

Figure 4   *Common critical evaluation cluster*

Gestures in Context

In addition to looking for gesture clusters and congruence of speech and body movement, all gestures should be considered in the context in which they occur. If, for example, someone was sitting at a bus terminal with arms and legs tightly crossed and chin down and it was a chilly winter's day, it would most likely mean that he or she was cold, not defensive. If, however, the person used the same gestures while you were sitting across a table from him trying to sell him an idea, product or service, they could be correctly interpreted as meaning that the person was negative or defensive about the situation.

Throughout this book all gestures will be considered in context and, where possible, gesture clusters will be examined.

Other Factors Affecting Interpretation

A man who has a 'dead fish' handshake is likely to be accused of having a weak character and the chapter on handshake techniques will explore the reason for this popular theory. But if a man has arthritis in his hands, it is likely that he will use a 'dead fish' handshake to avoid the pain of a strong one. Similarly, artists, musicians, surgeons and those in vocations whose work is delicate and involves use of their hands generally prefer not to shake hands, but, if they are forced to do so, they may use a 'dead fish' to protect them.

Someone who wears ill-fitting or tight clothing may be unable to use certain gestures, and this can affect use of body language. This applies to a minority of people, but it is important to consider what effect a person's physical restrictions or disabilities may have on his or her body movement.

Status and Power

Research in the field of linguistics has shown that there is a direct relationship between the amount of status, power or prestige a person commands and that person's range of vocabulary. In other words, the higher up the social or management ladder a person is, the better able he is to communicate in words and phrases. Non-verbal research has revealed a correlation between a person's command of the spoken word and the amount of gesticulation that that person uses to communicate his or her message. This means that a person's status, power or prestige is also directly related to the number of gestures or body movements he uses. The person at the top end of the social or management scale can use his range of words to communicate his meaning, whereas the less educated or unskilled person will rely more on gestures than words to communicate.

Throughout this book, most of the examples given refer to white, middle-class people but, as a general rule the higher the person on the socio-economic scale, the less gesticulation and body movement he uses.

The speed of some gestures and how obvious they look to others is also related to the age of the individual. For example, if a five-year-old child tells a lie to his or her parent, the mouth will be deliberately covered with one or both hands immediately afterwards (Figure 5). The gesture of covering the mouth alerts the parent to the lie and this gesture continues to be used throughout the individual's lifetime, usually varying only in the speed at which it is done. When the teenager tells a lie, the hand is brought to the mouth like that of a five-year-old, but instead of the obvious handslapping gesture over the mouth, the fingers rub lightly around it (Figure 6).

This mouth-covering gesture becomes even more refined in adulthood. When the adult tells a lie, his brain instructs his hand to cover his mouth in an attempt to block the deceitful words, just as it does for the five-year-old and the teenager, but at the last moment the hand is pulled away from the face and a nose touch gesture results (Figure 7). This gesture is nothing more than the adult's sophisticated version of the mouth-covering gesture that was used in childhood. This is an example of the fact that, as an individual gets older, many of his gestures become sophisticated and less obvious, which is why it is often more difficult to read the gestures of a fifty-year-old than those of a much younger person.

Figure 5 *The child telling a lie*

Figure 6 *The teenager*   **Figure 7** *The adult*
            telling a lie   *telling a lie*

Faking Body Language

A commonly asked question is, 'Is it possible to fake your own body language?' The general answer to this question is 'no' because of the lack of congruence that is likely to occur in the use of the main gestures, the body's microsignals and the spoken words. For example, open palms are associated with honesty but when the faker holds his palms out and smiles at you as he tells a lie, his microgestures give him away. His pupils may contract, one eyebrow may lift or the corner of his mouth may twitch, and these signals contradict the open palm gesture and the sincere smile. The result is that the receiver tends not to believe what he hears.

The human mind seems to possess a fail-safe mechanism

that registers 'tilt' when it receives a series of incongruent non-verbal messages. There are, however, some cases in which body language is deliberately faked to gain certain advantages. Take, for example, the Miss America or Miss Universe contest, in which each contestant uses studiously learned body movements to give the impression of warmth and sincerity. To the extent that each contestant can convey these signals, she will score points from the judges, but even the experts can only fake body language for a short period of time and eventually the body will emit signals that are independent of conscious actions. Many politicians are experts in faking body language in order to get the voters to believe what they are saying and the politician who can successfully do this is said to have 'charisma'.

The face is used more often than any other part of the body to cover up lies. We use smiles, nods and winks in an attempt to cover up, but unfortunately for us, our body signals tell the truth and there is a lack of congruence between our body gestures and facial signals. The study of facial signals is an art in itself. Little space is devoted to it in this book and for more information about it I recommend *Face Language* by Robert L. Whiteside and *Reading Faces* by Leopold Bellak, M.D., and Samm Sinclair Baker.

In summary, it is difficult to fake body language for a long period of time but, as we shall discuss, it is good to learn and to use positive, open gestures to communicate with others and to eliminate gestures that may give negative signals. This can make it more comfortable to be with people and can make you more acceptable to them.

How to Tell Lies Successfully

The difficulty with lying is that the subconscious mind acts automatically and independently of our verbal lie, so our body language gives us away. This is why people who rarely tell lies are easily caught, regardless of how convincing they may sound. The moment they begin to lie, the body sends out contradictory signals, and these give us our feeling that they are not telling the truth. During the lie, the subconscious mind sends out nervous energy that appears as a gesture that can contradict what the person said. Some people whose jobs involve lying, such as politicians, lawyers, actors and television announcers, have refined their body gestures to the point where it is difficult to 'see' the lie, and people fall for it, hook, line and sinker.

They refine their gestures in one of two ways. First, they practice what 'feel' like the right gestures when they tell the lie, but this is only successful when they have practiced telling numerous lies over long periods of time. Second, they can eliminate most gestures so that they do not use any positive or negative gestures while lying, but this is also very difficult to do.

Try this simple test when an occasion presents itself. Tell a deliberate lie to an acquaintance and make a conscious effort to suppress all body gestures while your body is in full view of the other person. Even when your major body gestures are consciously suppressed, numerous microgestures will still be transmitted. These include facial muscular twitching, expansion and contraction of pupils, sweating at the brow, flushing of the cheeks, increased rate of eye blinking and numerous other minute gestures that signal deceit. Research using slow motion cameras shows that these microgestures can occur within a split second and it is only people such as professional interviewers, salespeople and those whom we call perceptive who can consciously see them during a conversation or negotiation. The best interviewers and salespeople are those who have developed the unconscious ability to read the microgestures during face-to-face encounters.

It is obvious, then, that to be able to lie successfully, you must have your body hidden or out of sight. This is why police interrogation involves placing the suspect on a chair in the open or placing him under lights with his body in full view of the interrogators; his lies are much easier to see under those circumstances. Naturally, telling lies is easier if you are sitting behind a desk where your body is partially hidden, or while peering over a fence or behind a closed door. The best way to lie is over the telephone!

How to Learn Body Language

Set aside at least fifteen minutes a day to study and read the gestures of other people, as well as acquiring a conscious awareness of your own gestures. A good reading ground is anywhere that people meet and interact. An airport is a particularly good place for observing the entire spectrum of human gestures, as people openly express eagerness, anger, sorrow, happiness, impatience and many other emotions through gestures. Social functions, business meetings and parties are also excellent. Having studied the art of body language, you can go to a party, sit alone in a corner all evening like a wallflower and have an exciting time just watching other people's body language rituals! Television also offers an excellent way of learning non-verbal communication. Turn down the sound and try to understand what is happening by first watching the picture. By turning the sound up every five minutes, you will be able to check how accurate your non-verbal readings are and before long it will be possible to watch an entire program without any sound and understand what is happening, just as deaf people do.

Two

Territories and Zones

Thousands of books and articles have been written about the staking out and guarding of territories by animals, birds, fish and primates, but only in recent years has it been discovered that man also has territories. When this is learned and the implications understood, not only can enormous insights into one's own behavior and that of others be gained but the face-to-face reactions of others can be predicted. American anthropologist Edward T. Hall was one of the pioneers in the study of man's spatial needs and in the early 1960s he coined the word 'proxemics' (from 'proximity' or nearness). His research into this field has led to new understanding about our relationships with our fellow humans.

Every country is a territory staked out by clearly defined boundaries and sometimes protected by armed guards. Within each country are usually smaller territories in the form of states and counties. Within these are even smaller territories called cities, within which are suburbs, containing many streets that, in themselves, represent a closed territory to those who live there. The inhabitants of each territory share an intangible allegiance to it and have been known to turn to savagery and killing in order to protect it.

A territory is also an area or space that a person claims as his own, as if it were an extension of his body. Each person has his own personal territory which includes the area that exists around his possessions, such as his home which is bounded by fences, the inside of his motor vehicle, his own bedroom or personal chair and, as Dr. Hall discovered, a defined air space around his body.

This chapter will deal mainly with the implications of this air space and how people react when it is invaded.

Personal Space

Most animals have a certain air space around their bodies that they claim as their personal space. How far the space extends is mainly dependent on how crowded were the conditions in which the animal was raised. A lion raised in the remote regions of Africa may have a territorial air space with a radius of thirty-one miles or more, depending on the density of the lion population in that area, and it marks its territorial boundaries by urinating or defecating around them. On the other hand, a lion raised in captivity with other lions may have a personal space of only several feet, the direct result of crowded conditions.

Like the other animals, man has his own personal portable 'air bubble' that he carries around with him and its size is dependent on the density of the population in the place where he grew up. This personal zone distance is therefore culturally determined. Where some cultures, such as the Japanese, are accustomed to crowding, others prefer the 'wide open spaces' and like to keep their distance. However, we are mainly concerned with the territorial behavior of people raised in Western cultures.

Status can also have an effect on the distance at which a person stands in relation to others and this will be discussed in a later chapter.

Zone Distances

The radius of the air bubble around suburban middle-class white people living in North America, England, and Australia is generally the same. It can be broken down into four distinct zone distances.

1. *Intimate Zone* (between 15-46 cms)

Of all the zone distances, this is by far the most important as it is this zone that a person guards as if it were his own property. Only those who are emotionally close to that person are permitted to enter it. This includes lovers, parents, spouse, children, close friends and relatives. There is a sub-zone that extends up to 15 cms from the body that can be entered only during physical contact. This is the close intimate zone.

2. *Personal Zone* (between 46 cms and 1.2 metres)

This is the distance that we stand from others at cocktail parties, office parties, social functions and friendly gatherings.

3. *Social Zone* (1.2 to 3.6 metres)

We stand at this distance from strangers, the plumber or carpenter doing repairs around our home, the postman, the new employee at work and people whom we do not know very well.

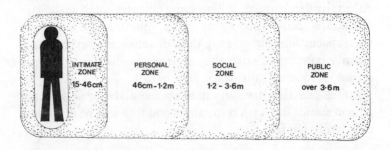

Figure 8 *Zone distances*

4. *Public Zone* (over 3.6 metres)
Whenever we address a large group of people, this is the comfortable distance at which we choose to stand.

Practical Applications of Zone Distances

Our intimate zone is normally entered by another person for one of two reasons. First, the intruder is a close relative or friend, or he or she may be making sexual advances. Second, the intruder is hostile and may be about to attack. While we will tolerate strangers moving within our personal and social zones, the intrusion of a stranger into our intimate zone causes physiological changes to take place within our bodies. The heart pumps faster, adrenaline pours into the bloodstream and blood is pumped to the brain and the muscles as physical preparations for a possible fight or flight situation.

This means that putting your arm in a friendly way on or around someone you have just met may result in that person's feeling negative towards you, even though he or she may smile and appear to enjoy it so as not to offend you. If you want people to feel comfortable in your company, the golden rule is 'keep your distance'. The more intimate our relationship is with other people, the closer we are permitted to move within their zones. For example, a new employee may initially feel that the other staff members are cold towards him, but they are only keeping him at the social zone distance until they know him better. As he becomes better known to the other employees, the territorial distance between him and them decreases until eventually he is permitted to move within their personal zones and, in some cases, their intimate zones.

The distance that two people who are kissing keep their hips apart can tell you something about the relationship that exists between them. Lovers press their torsos hard against each other and move within each other's close intimate zones. This differs from the kiss received from a stranger on New Year's Eve or from your best friend's spouse, both of whom keep their pelvic area at least 15 cm away from yours.

One of the exceptions to the distance/intimacy rule occurs where the spatial distance is based on the person's social standing. For example, the managing director of a company may be the weekend fishing buddy of one of his subordinates and when they go fishing each may move within the other's personal or intimate zone. At the office, however, the managing director keeps his fishing buddy at the social distance to maintain the unwritten social strata rules.

Crowding at concerts, movies, in elevators, trains or buses results in unavoidable intrusion into other people's intimate zones, and reactions to this invasion are interesting to observe. There is a list of unwritten rules that people in Western cultures follow rigidly when faced with a crowded situation such as a packed elevator or bus. These rules include:

1. You are not permitted to speak to anyone, including a person you know.
2. You must avoid eye contact with others at all times.
3. You are to maintain a 'poker face'—no emotion is permitted to be displayed.
4. If you have a book or newspaper, you must appear to be deeply engrossed in it.
5. The bigger the crowd, the less the body movement you are permitted to make.
6. In elevators, you are compelled to watch the floor numbers above your head.

We often hear words like 'miserable', 'unhappy' and 'despondent' used to describe people who travel to work in the rush hour on the bus. These labels are used because of the blank, expressionless look on the faces of the travelers, but they are misjudgments on the part of the observer. What the observer sees, in fact, is a group of people adhering to the rules that apply to the unavoidable invasion of their intimate zones in a crowded public place.

If you doubt this, notice how you behave next time you go alone to a crowded movie. As the usher directs you to your seat which is surrounded by a sea of unknown faces, notice how you will, like a pre-programmed robot, begin to obey the unwritten rules of behavior in crowded public places. As you begin to compete for territorial rights to the armrest with the unknown person beside you, you will begin to realize why those who go to a crowded movie alone often do not take their seats until the lights are turned down and the movie actually begins. Whether we are in a crowded elevator, movie or bus, people around us become non-persons—that is, they do not exist, as far as we are concerned and so we do not respond as if we were being attacked should someone inadvertently encroach upon our intimate territory.

An angry mob or group of protesters fighting for a mutual purpose does not react in the same way as do individuals when their territory is invaded; in fact, something quite different occurs. As the density of the crowd increases, each individual has less personal space and takes a hostile stance, which is why, as the size of the mob increases, it becomes angrier and uglier and fighting may begin to take place. This information is used by the police, who will try to break up the crowd so that each person can regain his own personal space and so become calmer.

Only in recent years have governments and town planners given any credence to the effect that high-density housing projects have in depriving individuals of their personal territory. The consequences of high-density living and overcrowding were seen in a recent study of the deer population on James Island, an island off the coast of Maryland. Many of the deer were dying in large numbers, despite the fact that at the time there was plenty of food, predators were not in evidence and infection was not present. Similar studies in earlier years with rats and rabbits revealed the same trend and further investigation showed that the deer had died as a result of overactive adrenal glands, resulting from the stress caused by the deprivation of each deer's personal territory as the population increased. The adrenal glands play an important part in the regulation of growth, reproduction and the level of the body's defenses. Thus overpopulation caused a physiological reaction to the stress; not other factors such as starvation, infection or aggression from others.

In view of this it is easy to see why areas that have the highest density of human population also have the highest crime and violence rates.

Police interrogators use territorial invasion techniques to break down the resistance of criminals being questioned. They seat the criminal on an armless, fixed chair in an open area of the room and encroach into his intimate and close intimate zones when asking questions, remaining there until he answers. It often takes only a short while for this territorial harassment to break down the criminal's resistance.

Management people can use this same approach to extract information from subordinates who may be withholding it, but a salesperson would be foolish to use this type of approach when dealing with customers.

Spacing Rituals

When a person claims a space or an area among strangers, such as a seat at the theater, a place at the conference table or a towel hook at the tennis court, he does it in a very predictable manner. He usually looks for the widest space available between two others and claims the area in the center. At the theater he will choose a seat that is halfway between the end of a row and where the nearest person is sitting. At the tennis courts, he chooses the towel hook that is in the largest available space, midway between two other towels or midway between the nearest towel and the end of the towel rack. The purpose of this ritual is not to offend the other people by being either too close or too far away from them.

At the theater, if you choose a seat more than halfway between the end of the row and the nearest other person, that other person may feel offended if you are too far away from him or he may feel intimidated if you sit too close, so the main purpose of this spacing ritual is to maintain harmony.

An exception to this rule is the spacing that occurs in public toilet blocks. Research shows that people choose the end toilets about 90 percent of the time and, if they are occupied, the midway principle is used.

Cultural Factors Affecting Zone Distances

A young couple who recently migrated from Denmark to live in Chicago were invited to join the local branch of the Jaycees. Some weeks after their admission to the club, several female members complained that the Danish man was making advances towards them, so that they felt uncomfortable in his presence and the male members of the club felt that the Danish woman had been indicating non-verbally that she would be sexually available to them.

This situation illustrates the fact that many Europeans have an intimate distance of only 23-25 cms and in some cultures it is even less. The Danish couple felt quite at ease and relaxed when standing at a distance of 25 cms from the Americans being totally unaware of their intrusion into the 18 inch intimate zone. The Danes also used eye gaze more frequently than the Americans, which gave rise to further misjudgments against them.

Moving into the intimate territory of someone of the opposite sex is a method that people use to show interest in that person and is commonly called an 'advance'. If the advance into the intimate zone is rejected, the other person will step backwards to maintain the zone distance. If the advance is accepted, the other person holds his or her ground and allows the intruder to remain within the intimate zone. What

Figure 9   *The acceptable conversational distance for most city dwellers*

seemed to the Danish couple to be a normal social encounter was being interpreted by the Americans as a sexual advance. The Danes thought the Americans were cold and unfriendly because they kept moving away to maintain the distance at which they felt comfortable.

At a recent conference, I noticed that when the Americans met and conversed, they stood at an acceptable 90 cms from each other and remained standing in the same place while talking. However, when a Japanese person spoke with an American, the two slowly began to move around the room, the American moving backwards away from the Japanese person and the Japanese person gradually moving towards the American. This was an attempt by both the American and Japanese person to adjust to a culturally comfortable distance

Figure 10 *The negative reaction of a woman on whose territory a man is encroaching. She is leaning backwards, attempting to maintain a comfortable distance. The problem is, however, that the man may be from a country with a smaller personal zone and is moving forward to stand at a distance that is comfortable for him. The woman may interpret this as a sexual move.*

from each other. The Japanese person, with his smaller 25 cms intimate zone, continually stepped forward to adjust to his spatial need, but by doing so he invaded the American's intimate space, causing him to step backwards to make his own spatial adjustment. Video recordings of this phenomenon replayed at high speed give the impression that both men are dancing around the conference room with the Japanese leading. It is therefore obvious why, when negotiating business, Asians and Americans look upon each other with some suspicion, the Americans referring to the Asians as 'pushy' and 'familiar' and the Asians referring to the Americans as 'cold', 'stand-offish' and 'cool'. The lack of awareness of the distance variation of the intimate zones in different cultures can easily lead to misconceptions and inaccurate assumptions about one culture by another.

Country vs. City Spatial Zones

As previously mentioned, the amount of personal space required by an individual is related to the population density of the area in which he was brought up. Those who were brought up in sparsely populated rural areas require more personal space than those raised in densely populated capital cities. Watching how far a person extends his arm to shake hands

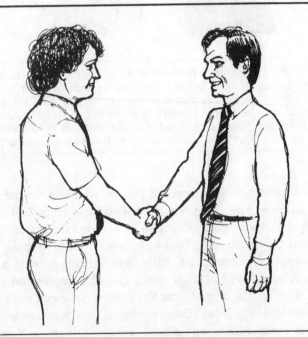

Figure 11 *Two men from the city greet each other*

can give a clue to whether he is from a major city or from a remote country area. City dwellers have their private 46 cms 'bubble'; this is also the measured distance between wrist and torso when they reach to shake hands (Figure 11). This allows the hand to meet the other person's on neutral territory. People brought up in a country town, where the population is far less dense, may have a territorial 'bubble' of up to 1.2 metres or more and this is the average measured distance from the wrist to the body when the person from the country is shaking hands (Figure 12).

Country people have a tendency to stand with their feet firmly planted on the ground and to lean forward as far as they can to meet your handshake, whereas a city dweller will step forward to greet you. People raised in remote or sparsely populated areas usually have a large personal space requirement

Figure 12   *Two men from a country town*

which may be as wide as 9 metres. These people refer not to shake hands but would rather stand at a distance and wave (Figure 13).

Figure 13 *People from a sparsely populated area*

City salespeople find this sort of information particularly useful for calling on farmers in sparse rural areas to sell farming equipment. Considering that the farmer may have a 'bubble' of 92 cms-1.8 metres or more, a handshake could be a territorial intrusion, causing the farmer to react negatively and be on the defensive. Successful country salespeople state almost unanimously that the best negotiating conditions exist when they greet the country town dweller with an extended handshake and the farmer in an isolated area with a distant wave.

Territory and Ownership

Property owned by a person or a place regularly used by him constitutes a private territory and, like personal air space, he will fight to protect it. Such things as a person's home, office and car represent a territory, each having clearly marked boundaries in the form of walls, gates, fences and doors. Each territory may have several sub-territories. For example, in a home a woman's private territory may be her kitchen and laundry and she objects to anyone invading that space when she is using it, a businessman has his favorite place at the conference table, diners have their favorite seat in the cafeteria and father has his favorite chair at home. These areas are usually marked either by leaving personal possessions on or around the area, or by frequent use of it. The cafeteria diner may even go so far as to carve his initials into 'his' place at the table and the businessman marks his territory at the conference table with such items as an ashtray, pens, books and clothing spread around his 46 cms intimate zone border. Dr. Desmond Morris noted that studies carried out in seating positions in libraries show that leaving a book or personal object on a library desk reserved that place for an average of seventy-seven minutes; leaving a jacket over a chair reserved it for two hours. At home a family member might mark his or her favorite chair by leaving a personal object, such as a pipe or magazine, on or near it to show his or her claim and ownership of the space.

If the head of the house asks a salesperson to be seated and the salesperson quite innocently sits in 'his' chair, the prospective buyer can become inadvertently agitated about this invasion of his territory and thus be put on the defensive. A simple question such as, 'Which chair is yours?', can avoid the negative results of making such a territorial error.

Motor Vehicles

Psychologists have noted that people driving cars react in a manner that is often completely unlike their normal social behavior as regards their territories. It seems that a car sometimes has a magnifying effect on the size of a person's personal space. In some cases, their territory is magnified by up to ten times the normal size, so the driver feels that he has a claim to an area of 3.7 to 4.6 metres in front of and behind his car.

When another driver cuts in front of him, even if no danger is involved, the driver may go through a physiological change, becoming angry and even attacking the other driver. Compare this to the situation that occurs when the same man is stepping into an elevator and another person steps in front of him, invading his personal territory. His reaction in those circumstances is normally apologetic and he allows the other man to go first; remarkably different from what happens when another driver cuts in front of him on the open road.

For some people, the car becomes a protective cocoon in which they can hide from the outside world. As they drive slowly beside the curb, almost in the gutter, they can be as big a hazard on the road as the driver with the expanded personal space.

In summary, others will invite or reject you, depending on the respect that you have for their personal space. This is why the happy-go-lucky person who slaps everyone he meets on the back or continually touches people during a conversation is secretly disliked by everyone. As a number of factors can affect the spatial distance a person takes in relation to others, it is wise to consider every criterion before making a judgment about why a person is keeping a certain distance.

From Figure 14, it is now possible to make any one of the following assumptions:

1. Both the man and woman are city dwellers and the man is making an intimate approach to the woman.
2. The man has a narrower intimate zone than the woman and is innocently invading hers.
3. The man is from a culture with a narrow intimate zone and the woman was brought up in a rural area.

A few simple questions and further observation of the couple can reveal the correct answer and help you avoid an embarrassing situation resulting from an incorrect assumption.

Figure 14 *Who is who and from where?*

Three

Palm Gestures

Openness and Honesty

Throughout history, the open palm has been associated with truth, honesty, allegiance and submission. Many oaths are taken with the palm of the hand over the heart, and the palm is held in the air when somebody is giving evidence in a court of law; the Bible is held in the left hand and the right palm held up for the members of the court to view.

In day-to-day encounters, people use two basic palm positions. The first has the palm facing upwards and is characteristic of the beggar asking for money or food. The second has the palm facing down as if it is holding down or restraining.

One of the most valuable ways of discovering whether someone is being open and honest or not is to look for palm displays. Just as a dog will expose its throat to show submission or surrender to the victor, so the human animal uses his or her palms to display the same attitude or emotion. For example, when people wish to be totally open or honest they will hold one or both palms out to the other person and say something like, 'Let me be completely open with you' (Figure 15). When someone begins to open up or be truthful, he will expose all or part of his palms to another person. Like most body language, this is a completely unconscious gesture, one that gives you a feeling or hunch that the other person is telling the truth. When a child is lying or concealing something, his palms are hidden behind his back. Similarly, a wife who wants to conceal her whereabouts after a night out with the girls will often hide her palms in her pockets or in an armfold position when she tries to explain where she was. Thus the hidden palms may give her husband a hunch that she is holding back the truth.

Figure 15 *'Let me be completely open with you.'*

Salespeople are often taught to look for the customer's exposed palms when he gives reasons why he cannot buy the product, because only valid reasons are given with exposed palms.

Intentional Use of Palms to Deceive

The reader may ask, 'Do you mean that if I tell lies with my palms visible, people will believe me?' The answer to this is yes—and no. If you tell an outright lie with your palms exposed, you may still appear insincere to your listeners because many of the other gestures that should also be visible when displaying honesty will be absent and the negative gestures used when lying will be visible and therefore inconsistent with the open palms. As already noted, con men and professional liars are people who have developed the special art of making their non-verbal signals complement their verbal lies. The more effectively the professional con man can use the non-verbal gestures of honesty when telling a lie, the better he is at his vocation.

It is possible, however, to make yourself appear more credible by practicing open palm gestures when communicating with others; conversely, as the open palm gestures become habitual, the tendency to tell untruths lessens. Interestingly, most people find it difficult to lie with their palms exposed and the use of palm signals can in fact help to suppress some of the false information others may give. It also encourages them to be open with you.

Palm Power

One of the least noticed but most powerful non-verbal signals is given by the human palm. When used correctly, palm power invests its user with a degree of authority and the power of silent command over others.

There are three main palm command gestures: the palm-up position, the palm-down position and the palm-closed-finger-pointed position. The differences of the three positions are shown in this example: let's say that you ask someone to pick up a box and carry it to another location in the same room. We assume that you use the same tone of voice, the same words and facial expressions, and change only the position of your palm.

The palm facing up is used as a submissive, non-threatening gesture, reminiscent of the pleading gesture of a street beggar. The person being asked to move the box will not feel that the request is given with pressure and, in a normal superior/subordinate situation, will not feel threatened by the request.

When the palm is turned to face downwards, you will have immediate authority. The person to whom you have directed the request feels that he has been given an order to remove the box and may feel antagonistic towards you, depending on your relationship with him. For example, if the person to whom you gave the request was a co-worker of equal status, he could reject your palm-down request and would be more likely to carry out your wish if you had used the palm-up position. If the person to whom you give the request is your subordinate, the palm-down gesture is acceptable, as you have the authority to use it.

In Figure 18, the palm is closed into a fist and the pointed finger becomes a symbolic club with which the speaker figuratively beats his listener into submission. The pointed finger is one of the most irritating gestures that a person can use while speaking, particularly when it beats time to the speaker's words. If you are an habitual finger-pointer, try practicing the palm-up and palm-down positions and you will find that you create a more relaxed attitude and have a more positive effect on other people.

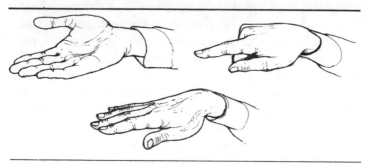

Figure 16
Submissive palm position

Figure 17
Dominant palm position

Figure 18
Aggressive palm position

Shaking Hands

Shaking hands is a relic of the caveman era. Whenever cavemen met, they would hold their arms in the air with their palms exposed to show that no weapons were being held or concealed. This palms-in-air gesture became modified over the centuries and such gestures as the palm raised in the air, the palm over the heart and numerous other variations developed. The modern form of this ancient greeting ritual is the interlocking and shaking of the palms which, in most English-speaking countries, is performed both on initial greeting and on departure. The hands are normally pumped three to seven times.

Dominant and Submissive Handshakes

Considering what has already been said about the impact of a command given in both the palm-up and palm-down positions, let us explore the relevance of these two palm positions in hand shaking.

Assume that you have just met someone for the first time and you greet each other with a customary handshake. One of three basic attitudes is transmitted through the handshake. These are dominance: 'This person is trying to dominate me. I'd better be cautious', submission: 'I can dominate this person. He will do as I wish', and equality: 'I like this person. We will get on well together'.

These attitudes are transmitted unconsciously and, with practice and conscious application, the following handshaking techniques can have an immediate effect on the outcome of a face-to-face encounter with another person. The information in this chapter represents one of the few documented studies of handshake control techniques.

Dominance is transmitted by turning your hand (dark shirt sleeve) so that your palm faces down in the handshake (Figure

19). Your palm need not be facing the floor directly, but should be facing downwards in relation to the other person's palm and this tells him that you wish to take control in the encounter that follows. Studies of fifty-four successful senior management people have revealed that not only did forty-two initiate the handshake, but they also used dominant handshake control.

Just as the dog shows submission by rolling on its back and exposing its throat to the aggressor, so the human uses the palm-up gesture to show submission to others. The reverse of the dominant handshake is to offer your hand with your palm facing upwards (Figure 20). This is particularly effective when you want to give the other person control or allow him to feel that he is in control of the situation.

However, though the palm-up handshake can show a submissive attitude, there may be mitigating circumstances to consider. For example, a person who has arthritis in the hands will be forced to give you a limp handshake because of his condition and this makes it easy to turn his palm into the submissive position. People who use their hands in their profession, such as surgeons, artists and musicians, may also give a limp handshake purely to protect their hands. The gestures that follow the handshake will give further clues for

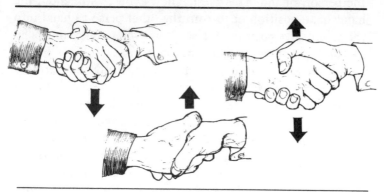

Figure 19 *Taking the control*   **Figure 20** *Giving the control*   **Figure 21** *'Shake like a man'*

your assessment of that person—the submissive person will use submissive gestures and the dominant person will use more aggressive gestures.

When two dominant people shake hands, a symbolic struggle takes place as each person tries to turn the other's palm into the submissive position. The result is a vice-like handshake with both palms remaining in the vertical position as each person transmits a feeling of respect and rapport to the other (Figure 21). This vice-like vertical palm grip is the handshake that a father teaches his son when he shows him how to 'shake hands like a man'.

When you receive a dominant handshake from another person, it is not only difficult to force his palm back over into the submissive position, but it becomes very obvious when you do it. There is a simple technique for disarming the dominant handshaker that, in addition to giving you back the control, can enable you to intimidate the other person by invading his personal space. To perfect this disarmament technique you need to practice stepping forward with your left foot as you reach to shake hands (Figure 23). Next, bring your right leg forward, moving left in front of the person and into his personal space (Figure 24). Now bring your left leg across to your right leg to complete the maneuver, then shake the person's hand. This tactic allows you to straighten the handshake position or to turn the other person's hand into the submissive position. It also allows you to take control by invading the other person's intimate zone.

Analyze your own approach to shaking hands to determine whether you step forward on your left or right foot when you extend your arm to shake hands. Most people are right-footed and are therefore at a great disadvantage when they receive a dominant handshake, as they have little flexibility or room to move within the confines of the handshake and it allows the other person to take the control. Practice stepping into a handshake with your left foot and you will find that it is quite simple to neutralize a dominant handshake and take the control.

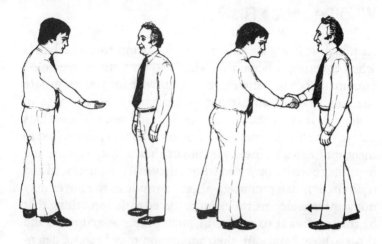

Figure 22 *The man on the right is presented with a dominant handshake.*

Figure 23 *He takes the handshake and steps forward on his left foot.*

Figure 24 *He brings his right foot across and moves into the other man's intimate zone, bringing the handshake into a vertical position.*

Who Reaches First?

Although it is a generally accepted custom to shake hands when meeting a person for the first time, there are some circumstances in which it may be unwise for you to initiate the handshake. Considering that a handshake is a sign of welcome, it is important to ask yourself several questions before you initiate one: Am I welcome? Is this person glad to meet me? Sales trainees are taught that, if they initiate the handshake with a buyer on whom they call unannounced and uninvited, it can produce a negative result as the buyer may not want to welcome them and is forced to do something that he may not want to do. Again, such people as arthritics and those whose hands are their profession may become defensive if they are forced to shake hands. Under these circumstances, sales trainees are told that it is better to wait for the other person to initiate the handshake and, if it is not forthcoming, to nod as a sign of greeting.

Handshake Styles

The palm-down thrust is certainly the most aggressive handshake style as it gives the receiver little chance of establishing an equal relationship. This handshake is typical of the aggressive, dominant male who always initiates it, and the stiff arm with palm facing directly downwards forces the receiver into the submissive position because he has to respond with his palm facing up.

Several ways to counter the palm-down thrust have been developed. You can use the step-to-the-right technique (Figures 22 to 24), but sometimes this is difficult to use as the initiator's arm is often tense and stiff to prevent such tactics. A simple maneuver is to grasp the person's hand on top and then shake it (Figure 26). With this approach, you become the dominant party, as you not only have control of the other person's hand, but yours is in the superior position on top of his with your palm facing down. As this can be embarrassing to the aggressor, we suggest that it be used with caution and discretion.

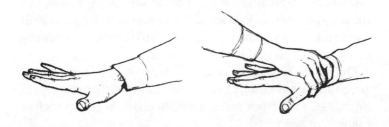

Figure 25 *Palm-down thrust*   **Figure 26** *Disarming the palm-down thrust*

The glove handshake is sometimes called the politician's handshake. The initiator tries to give the receiver the impression that he is trustworthy and honest, but when this technique is used on a person he has just met, it has the reverse effect. The receiver feels suspicious and cautious about the initiator's intentions. The glove should only be used with people to whom the initiator is well-known.

Figure 27 *The glove*

Few greeting gestures are as uninviting as the dead fish handshake, particularly when the hand is cold or clammy. The soft, placid feel of the dead fish makes it universally unpopular and most people relate it to weak character, mainly because of the ease with which the palm can be turned up. Surprisingly, many people who use the dead fish are unaware that they do so, and it is wise to ask your friends to comment on your own handshake delivery before deciding which style you will use in the future.

The knuckle grinder is the trademark of the aggressive 'tough guy' type. Unfortunately, there are no effective ways to counter it, apart from verbal abuse or physical action such as a punch in the nose!

Figure 28 *The knuckle grinder*

Like the palm-down thrust, the stiff-arm thrust tends to be used by aggressive types and its main purpose is to keep you at a distance and out of the initiator's intimate zone. It is also used by people brought up in country areas who have a larger intimate zone to protect their personal territory. With country folk, however, there is a tendency to lean forward or even balance on one foot when delivering the stiff-arm thrust.

Figure 29 *The stiff-arm thrust*

The finger-tip grab is like the stiff-arm thrust that has missed the mark; the user mistakenly grabs the other person's fingers. Even though the initiator may appear to have a keen and enthusiastic attitude toward the receiver, in fact he lacks confidence in himself. Like the stiff-arm thrust, the main aim of the finger-tip grab is to keep the receiver at a comfortable spatial distance.

Figure 30   *The fingertip grab*

Pulling the receiver into the initiator's territory can mean one of two things: first, the initiator is an insecure type who feels safe only within his own personal space or second, the initiator is from a culture that has a small intimate zone and he is behaving normally.

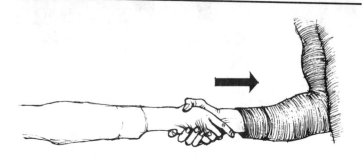

Figure 31   *The arm-pull*

The intention of the double-handed handshake is to show sincerity, trust or depth of feeling towards the receiver. Two significant elements should be noticed. Firstly, the left hand is used to communicate the extra feeling that the initiator wishes to transmit and its extent is related to the distance that the initiator's left hand is moved up the receiver's right arm. The elbow grasp, for example (Figure 33), transmits more feeling than the wrist hold (Figure 32), and the shoulder hold (Figure 35) transmits more than the upper-arm grip (Figure 34). Secondly, the initiator's left hand represents an invasion of the receiver's intimate and close intimate zones. In general, the wrist hold and the elbow grasp are acceptable only between close friends or relatives and in these cases, the initiator's left hand penetrates only the receiver's intimate zone. The shoulder hold (Figure 35) and the upper-arm grip (Figure 34) enter the receiver's close intimate zone and may involve actual body contact. They should be used only between people who experience a close emotional bond at the time of the handshake. Unless the extra feeling is mutual or the initiator has a good reason for using a double-handed handshake, the receiver will become suspicious and mistrust the initiator's

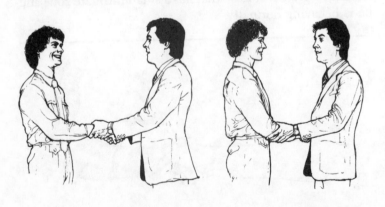

Figure 32 *The wrist hold*   **Figure 33** *The elbow grasp*

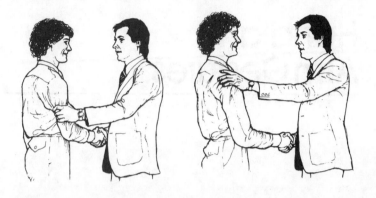

Figure 34 *The upper-arm grip*   **Figure 35** *The shoulder hold*

intentions. It is quite common to see politicians greeting voters and salespeople meeting their new customers with a double-handed handshake without realizing that this can be social suicide, putting the receiver off.

Four

Hand and Arm Gestures

Hand Gestures

Rubbing the Palms Together

Recently a personal friend of ours visited my wife and I at our home to discuss the details of an upcoming skiing vacation. In the course of the conversation our friend suddenly sat back in her chair, smiled broadly, rubbed her palms together and exclaimed, 'I can hardly wait to go!' Non-verbally she had told us that she expected the trip to be a big success.

Rubbing the palms together is a way in which people non-verbally communicate positive expectation. The dice-thrower rubs the dice between his palms as a sign that he expects to win, the master of ceremonies rubs his palms together and says to his audience, 'We have long looked forward to hearing our next speaker', and the excited salesperson struts into the sales manager's office, rubs his palms together and says excitedly, 'We've just got a big order, boss!' However, the waiter who comes to your table at the end of the evening rubbing his palms together and asking, 'Anything else, sir?' is non-verbally telling you that he is expecting a tip.

The speed at which a person rubs his palms together signals

Figure 36   *'Isn't it exciting!'*

whom he thinks will receive the positive results that are expected. Say, for example, you want to buy a home and you go to see a real estate agent. After describing the property you are seeking, the agent rubs his palms together quickly and says, 'I've got just the right place for you!' The agent has signaled that he expects the results to be to *your* benefit. But how would you feel if he rubbed his palms together very slowly as he told you that he had the ideal property? He would then appear to be crafty or devious and would give you the feeling that the expected results would be to *his* advantage rather than yours. Salespeople are taught that if they use the palm-rub gesture when describing products or services to prospective buyers, they should be certain to use a fast hand action to avoid putting the buyer on the defensive. When the buyer rubs his palms together and says to the salesperson, 'Let's see what you have to offer!' it is a signal that the buyer is expecting to be shown something good and is likely to make a purchase.

A word of warning: a person who is standing at a bus terminal in freezing winter conditions and who rubs his palms together briskly may not necessarily be doing this because he is expecting a bus. He does it because his hands are cold!

Thumb and Finger Rub

Rubbing the thumb against the fingertips or against the index finger is commonly used as a money expectancy gesture. It is often used by salespeople who rub their fingertips and thumb together and say to their customers 'I can save you 40 percent', or the person who rubs his index finger and thumb together and says to his friend, 'Lend me ten dollars'. This is obviously a gesture that should be avoided at all times by a professional person when dealing with his clients.

Hands Clenched Together

At first this seems to be a confidence gesture as people who use it are often smiling and sound happy. However, on one particular occasion, we saw a salesperson describing the sale he had just lost. As he went further and further into his story, we noticed that not only had he taken the hands-clenched position, but his fingers were beginning to turn white and they looked as though they were welding together. This was therefore a gesture showing a frustrated or hostile attitude.

Research by Nierenberg and Calero on the hands-clenched position brought them to the conclusion that this was a frustration gesture, signaling that the person was holding back a negative attitude. The gesture has three main positions; hands clenched in front of the face (Figure 37), hands resting on the desk (Figure 38) or on the lap when seated and placed in front of the crotch when standing (Figure 39).

Figure 37   *Hands clenched in raised position*

There also appears to be a correlation between the height at which the hands are held and the strength of the person's negative mood; that is, the person would be more difficult to handle when the hands are held high as in Figure 37 than he would be with the Figure 38 position. Like all negative gestures, some action needs to be taken to unlock the person's fingers to expose the palms and the front of the body, or the hostile attitude will remain.

Figure 38   *Hands clenched in middle position*

Figure 39   *Hands clenched in lower position*

Steepling Hands

I stated at the beginning of this book that gestures come in clusters, like words in a sentence, and that they must be interpreted in the context in which they are observed. 'Steepling', as Birdwhistell called it, can be an exception to these rules, as it is often used in isolation from other gestures. In fact, people who are confident, superior types or who use minimal or restricted body gestures often use this gesture, and, by doing so, they signal their confident attitude.

My observation and research into this fascinating gesture show that it is frequently used in superior/subordinate interaction and that it can be an isolated gesture which indicates a confident or 'know-it-all' attitude. Managers often use this gesture position when giving instructions or advice to subordinates and it is particularly common among accountants, lawyers, managers and the like.

The gesture has two versions; the raised steeple (Figure 40), the position normally taken when the steepler is giving his opinions or ideas and is doing the talking. The lowered-steeple gesture (Figure 41) is normally used when the steepler is listening rather than speaking. Nierenberg and Calero noted that women tend to use the lowered-steeple position more often than the raised-steeple position. When the raised-steeple position is taken with the head tilted back, the person assumes an air of smugness or arrogance.

Although the steeple gesture is a positive signal, it can be used in either positive or negative circumstances and may be misinterpreted. For example, a salesman presenting his product to a potential buyer may have observed several positive gestures given by the buyer during the interview. These could include open palms, leaning forward, head up and so on. Let's say that towards the end of the sales presentation the customer takes one of the steeple positions.

If the steeple follows a series of other positive gestures, appearing when the salesman shows the buyer the solution to

Figure 40   *The raised steeple*

Figure 41   *The lowered steeple*

his problem, the salesman has been given a cue to close the sale, ask for the order and expect to get it. On the other hand, if the steeple gesture follows a series of negative gestures such as arm folding, leg crossing, looking away and numerous hand-to-face gestures, and if the buyer takes the steeple position towards the close of the sales presentation, the buyer may be confident that he will not buy or that he can get rid of the salesman. In both these cases the steeple gesture means confidence, but one has positive results and the other negative consequences for the salesman. The movements preceding the steeple gesture are the key to the outcome.

Gripping Hands, Arms and Wrists

Several prominent male members of the British Royal Family are noted for their habit of walking with their head up, chin out and one palm gripping the other hand behind the back. Not only does British Royalty use this gesture; it is common among Royalty of many countries. On the local scene, the gesture is used by the policeman patrolling his beat, the principal of the local school when he is walking through the school yard, senior military personnel and others in positions of authority.

This is therefore a superiority/confidence gesture position. It also allows the person to expose his vulnerable stomach, heart and throat regions to others in an unconscious act of fearlessness. Our own experience shows that, if you take this position when you are in a high-stress situation, such as being interviewed by newspaper reporters or simply waiting outside a dentist's office, you will feel quite relaxed, confident and even authoritative.

Our observations show that police officers who wear firearms seldom display this gesture, but use the hands-on-hips aggressive gesture, (Figure 95). It seems that the firearm itself

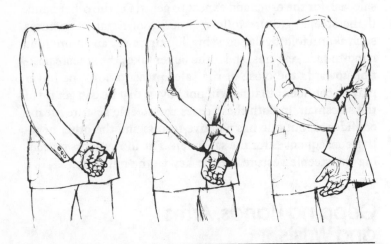

Figure 42
The superiority confidence gesture

Figure 43
The hand-gripping-wrist gesture

Figure 44
The upper arm grip

has sufficient authority for its wearer so that the palm-in-palm gesture becomes unnecessary as a display of authority.

The palm-in-palm gesture should not be confused with the hand-gripping-wrist gesture (Figure 43) which is a signal of frustration and an attempt at self-control. In this case one hand grips the other wrist or arm very tightly as if it is an attempt by one arm to prevent the other from striking out.

Interestingly, the further the hand is moved up the back, the more angry the person has become. The man in Figure 44, for example, is showing a greater attempt at self-control than the man in Figure 43 because the hand in Figure 44 is gripping the upper arm, not just the wrist. It is this type of gesture that has given rise to such expressions as, 'Get a good grip on yourself'. This gesture is often used by salespeople who have called on a potential buyer and have been asked to wait in the buyer's reception area. It is a poor attempt by the salesman to disguise his nervousness and an astute buyer is likely to sense this. If a self-control gesture is changed to the palm-in-palm position, a calming and confident feeling results.

Thumb Displays

In palmistry, the thumbs denote strength of character and ego and the non-verbal use of thumbs agrees with this. They are used to display dominance, superiority or even aggression; thumb gestures are secondary gestures, a supportive part of a gesture cluster. Thumb displays are positive signals, often used in the typical pose of the 'cool' manager who uses them in the presence of subordinates. A courting man uses them in the presence of a potential female partner and they are common among people who wear high-status or prestige cloth-

Figure 45 *The cardigan or vest thruster*

ing. People wearing new, attractive clothing use thumb displays more frequently than those who wear older, outdated clothing.

The thumbs, which display superiority, become most obvious when a person gives a contradictory verbal message. Take for example, the lawyer who turns to the jury and in a soft, low voice says, 'In my humble opinion, ladies and gentlemen of the jury . . .' while displaying dominant thumb gestures and tilting back his head to 'look down his nose' (Figure 46). This has the effect of making the jury feel that the lawyer is insincere, even pompous. If the lawyer wished to appear humble, he should have approached the jury with one foot toward them, his coat open, an open palm display and stooping forward a little to show humility, or even subordination to the jury.

Figure 46   *'In my humble opinion . . .'*

Thumbs most often protrude from people's pockets, sometimes from the back pockets (Figure 47) in a secretive manner to try to hide the person's dominant attitude. Women also use this gesture (Figure 48). In addition to all this, thumb thrusters will often rock on the balls of their feet to give the impression of extra height.

Figure 47 *Thumbs protruding from back pockets*

Figure 48 *The dominant female*

Arms folded with thumbs pointing upwards is another popular thumb-gesture position. This is a double signal, that of a defensive or negative attitude, (folded arms) plus a superior attitude (displayed by the thumbs). The person using this double gesture usually gesticulates with his or her thumbs, and rocking on the balls of the feet when standing is common.

Figure 49   *Thumbs-up position*

The thumb can also be used as a signal of ridicule or disrespect when it is used to point at another person. For example, the husband who leans across to his friend, points toward his wife with a closed-fist thumb-gesture and says, 'Women are all the same, you know', is inviting an argument with his wife. In this case the shaking thumb is used as a pointer to ridicule the unfortunate woman. Consequently, thumb-pointing is irritating to most women, particularly when a man does it. The shaking thumb is less common among women, although they sometimes use the gesture at people they do not like.

Figure 50   *'Women . . . they're all the same!'*

Five

Hand-to-Face Gestures

Deceit, Doubt, Lying

How can you tell when someone is lying? Recognition of the non-verbal deceit gestures can be one of the most important observation skills one can acquire. So what deceit signals can give people away?

One of the most commonly used symbols of deceit is that of the three wise monkeys who hear, speak and see no evil. The hand-to-face actions depicted form the basis of the human deceit gestures. In other words, when we see, speak and hear untruths or deceit, we often attempt to cover our mouth, eyes or ears with our hands. We have already mentioned that children use these obvious deceit gestures quite openly. If the young child tells a lie, he will often cover his mouth with his hands in an attempt to stop the deceitful words from coming out. If he does not wish to listen to a reprimanding parent, he simply covers his ears with his hands. When he sees something he doesn't wish to look at, he covers his eyes with his hands or arms. As a person becomes older, the hand-to-face gestures become more refined and less obvious but they still occur when a person is lying, covering up or witnessing deceit; deceit can also mean doubt, uncertainty, lying or exaggeration.

When someone uses a hand-to-face gesture, it does not

always mean that he or she is lying. It does, however, indicate that the person may be deceiving you and further observation of his other gesture clusters can confirm your suspicions. It is important that you do not interpret hand-to-face gestures in isolation.

Dr. Desmond Morris noted that researchers tested nurses who were instructed to lie to their patients about their health in a role-play situation. The nurses who lied showed a greater frequency of hand-to-face gestures than those who told the truth to the patients. This chapter looks at the variations in hand-to-face gestures and discusses how and when they occur.

The Mouth Guard

The mouth guard is one of the few adult gestures that is as obvious as a child's. The hand covers the mouth and the thumb is pressed against the cheek as the brain subconsciously instructs it to try and suppress the deceitful words that are being said. Sometimes this gesture may only be several fingers over the mouth or even a closed fist, but its meaning remains the same.

The mouth guard is not to be confused with evaluation gestures, which will be covered later in this chapter.

Many people try to disguise the mouth-guard gesture by giving a fake cough. When playing the role of a gangster or criminal, Humphrey Bogart often used this gesture when discussing criminal activities with other gangsters or when being interrogated by the police to show non-verbally that he was being dishonest.

If the person who is speaking uses this gesture, it indicates that he is telling a lie. If, however, he covers his mouth while you are speaking, it indicates that he feels *you* are lying! One of the most unsettling sights a public speaker can see is his audience all using this gesture while he is speaking. In a small audience or a one-to-one situation, it is wise to stop the pre-

Figure 51 *The mouth guard*

sentation or delivery and ask, 'Would someone care to comment on what I've just said?' This allows the audience's objections to be brought out into the open, giving you the opportunity to qualify your statements and to answer questions.

Nose Touching

In essence, the nose-touch gesture is a sophisticated, disguised version of the mouth-guard gesture. It may consist of several light rubs below the nose or it may be one quick, almost imperceptible touch. Some women perform this gesture with small discreet strokes to avoid smudging their make-up.

Figure 52   *The nose touch*

One explanation of the origin of the nose-touch gesture is that, as the negative thought enters the mind, the sub-conscious instructs the hand to cover the mouth, but, at the last moment, in an attempt to appear less obvious, the hand pulls away from the face and a quick nose-touch gesture is the result. Another explanation is that lying causes the delicate nerve endings in the nose to tingle, and the rubbing action takes place to satisfy this feeling. 'But what if the person only has an itchy nose?' is frequently asked. The itch in a person's nose is normally satisfied by a very deliberate rubbing or scratching action, as opposed to the light strokes of the nose-touch gesture. Like the mouth-guard gesture, it can be used both by the speaker to disguise his own deceit and by the listener who doubts the speaker's words.

The Eye Rub

'See no evil' says the wise monkey, and this gesture is the brain's attempt to block out the deceit, doubt or lie that it sees or to avoid having to look at the face of the person to whom he is telling the lie. Men usually rub their eyes vigorously and if the lie is a big one they will often look away, normally towards the floor. Women use a small, gentle rubbing motion just below the eye, either because they have been brought up to avoid making robust gestures, or to avoid smudging make-up. They also avoid a listener's gaze by looking at the ceiling.

Figure 53 *The eye rub*

'Lying through your teeth' is a common phrase. It refers to a gesture cluster of clenched teeth and a false smile, combined with the eye-rub gesture and an averted gaze. This gesture is used by movie actors to portray insincerity, but is rarely seen in real life.

The Ear Rub

This is, in effect, an attempt by the listener to 'hear no evil' in trying to block the words by putting the hand around or over the ear. This is the sophisticated adult version of the hands-over-both-ears gesture used by the young child who wants to block out his parent's reprimands. Other variations of the ear-rub gesture include rubbing the back of the ear, the finger drill (where the fingertip is screwed back and forth inside the ear), pulling at the earlobe or bending the entire ear forward to cover the earhole. This last gesture is a signal that the person has heard enough or may want to speak.

Figure 54   *The ear rub*

The Neck Scratch

In this case, the index finger of the writing hand scratches below the earlobe, or may even scratch the side of the neck. Our observation of this gesture reveals an interesting point: the person scratches about five times. Rarely is the number of scratches less than five and seldom more than five. This gesture is a signal of doubt or uncertainty and is characteristic of the person who says, 'I'm not sure I agree.' It is very noticeable when the verbal language contradicts it, for example, when the person says something like, 'I can understand how you feel.'

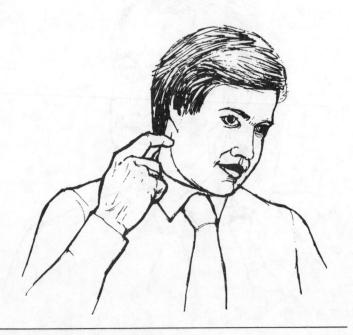

Figure 55   *The neck scratch*

The Collar Pull

Desmond Morris noted that research into the gestures of those who tell lies revealed that the telling of a lie caused a tingling sensation in the delicate facial and neck tissues and a rub or scratch was required to satisfy it. This seems to be a reasonable explanation of why some people use the collar-pull gesture when they tell a lie and suspect that they have been caught. It is almost as if the lie causes a slight trickle of sweat to form on the neck when the deceiver feels that you suspect he is lying. It is also used when a person is feeling angry or frustrated and needs to pull the collar away from his neck in an attempt to let the cool air circulate around it. When you see someone use this gesture, a question like, 'Would you repeat that, please?' or, 'Could you clarify that point, please?' can cause the would-be deceiver to give the game away.

Figure 56   *The collar pull*

Fingers in the Mouth

Morris's explanation of this gesture is that the fingers are placed in the mouth when a person is under pressure. It is an unconscious attempt by the person to revert to the security of the child sucking on his mother's breast. The young child substitutes his thumb for the breast and as an adult, he not only puts his fingers to his mouth but inserts such things as cigarettes, pipes, pens and the like into it. Whereas most hand-to-mouth gestures involve lying or deception, the fingers-in-mouth gesture is an outward manifestation of an inner need for reassurance. Giving the person guarantees and assurances is appropriate when this gesture appears (Figure 57).

Figure 57   *Reassurance is needed here*

Interpreting and Misinterpreting

The ability to accurately interpret hand-to-face gestures in a given set of circumstances takes considerable time and observation to acquire. We can confidently assume that, when a person uses one of the hand-to-face gestures just mentioned, a negative thought has entered his mind. The question is, what is the negative? It could be doubt, deceit, uncertainty, exaggeration, apprehension or outright lying. The real skill of interpretation is the ability to pick which of the negatives mentioned is the correct one. This can best be done by an analysis of the gestures preceding the hand-to-face gesture and interpreting it in context.

For example, a friend of mine with whom I play chess often rubs his ear or touches his nose during the game, but only when he is unsure of his next move. Recently I noticed some of his other gestures that I can interpret and use to my advantage. I have discovered that when I signal my intention to move a chess piece by touching it, he immediately uses gesture clusters that signal what he thinks about my proposed move. If he sits back in the chair and uses a steepling gesture (confidence), I can assume that he has anticipated my move and may already have thought of a counter move. If, as I touch my chess piece, he covers his mouth or rubs his nose or ear, it means that he is uncertain about my move, his next move or both. This means that the more moves I can make after he has reacted with a negative hand-to-face gesture, the greater my chances of winning.

I recently interviewed a young man for a position in our company. Throughout the interview he kept his arms and legs crossed, used critical evaluation clusters, had very little palm exposure and his gaze met mine less than one-third of the time. Something was obviously worrying him, but at that point in the interview I did not have sufficient information for an accurate assessment of his negative gestures. I asked him some questions about his previous employers. His answers were accompanied by a series of eye-rubbing and nose-touching gestures and he continued to avoid my gaze. This continued throughout the rest of the interview and eventually I decided not to hire him, based on what is commonly called 'gut feeling'. Being curious about his deceit gestures, I decided to check his references and discovered that he had given me false information about his past. Had I not been aware of non-verbal cues and signals, I might well have made the mistake of hiring him.

During a videotaped role-play of an interview scene at a management seminar, the interviewee suddenly covered his mouth and rubbed his nose after he had been asked a question by the interviewer. Up to that point in the role-play, the job applicant had kept an open posture with open coat, palms visible and leaning forward when answering questions, so at first we thought it might have been an isolated series of gestures. He displayed the mouth-guard gesture for several seconds before giving his answer, then returned to his open pose. We questioned him about the hand-to-mouth gesture at the end of the role play and he said that, when he had been asked the particular question, he could have responded in two ways; one negative, one positive. As he thought about the negative answer and of how the interviewer might react to it, the mouth-guard gesture occurred. When he thought of the positive answer, however, his hand dropped away from his mouth and he resumed his open posture. His uncertainty about the audience's possible reaction to the negative reply had caused the sudden mouth-guard gesture to occur.

These examples illustrate how easy it can be to misinterpret a hand-to-face gesture and to jump to wrong conclusions. It is only by constant study and observation of these gestures and by having regard to the context in which they occur that one can eventually learn to reach an accurate assessment of someone's thoughts.

Cheek and Chin Gestures

A good speaker is said to be one who 'instinctively' knows when his audience is interested in what he says and when his listeners have had enough. A good salesperson senses when he is hitting his client's 'hot buttons', that is, finding out where the buyer's interest lies. Every salesperson knows the empty feeling that results when he or she is giving a sales presentation to a potential buyer who says very little and just sits there watching. Fortunately a number of hand-to-cheek and hand-to-chin gestures can tell the salesperson how well he is doing.

Boredom

When the listener begins to use his hand to support his head, it is a signal that boredom has set in and his supporting hand

Figure 58 *Boredom*

is an attempt to hold his head up to stop himself from falling asleep. The degree of the listener's boredom is related to the extent to which his arm and hand are supporting his head. Extreme boredom and lack of interest are shown when the head is fully supported by the hand (Figure 58) and the ultimate boredom signal occurs when the head is on the desk or table and the person is snoring!

Drumming the fingers on the table and continual tapping of the feet on the floor are often misinterpreted by professional speakers as boredom signals, but in fact they signal impatience. When you as a speaker notice these signals, a strategic move must be made to get the finger drummer or foot tapper involved in your lecture, thus avoiding his negative effect on the other members of the audience. The audience who displays boredom and impatience signals together is telling the speaker that it is time for him to end the speech. It is worth noting that the speed of the finger tap or foot tap is related to the extent of the person's impatience—the faster the taps, the more impatient the listener is becoming.

Evaluation

Evaluation is shown by a closed hand resting on the cheek, often with the index finger pointing upwards (Figure 59). Should the person begin to lose interest but wish to appear interested, for courtesy's sake, the position will alter slightly so that the heel of the palm supports the head, as shown in Figure 58. I have attended numerous management meetings where the young up-and-coming managers have used this interest gesture to show respect to the company president who is giving a boring speech. Unfortunately for them, however, as soon as the hand supports the head in any way, it gives the game away and the president is likely to feel that some of the young managers are insincere or are using false flattery.

Figure 59   *Interested evaluation*

Genuine interest is shown when the hand is on the cheek, not used as a head support. An easy way for the president to gain their individual attention would be to say something like, 'I'm glad that you are paying attention because in a moment I'm going to ask questions!' This rivets his listeners' attention to his speech because of the fear that they will not be able to answer the questions.

When the index finger points vertically up the cheek and the thumb supports the chin, the listener is having negative or critical thoughts about the speaker or his subject. Often the index finger may rub or pull at the eye as the negative thoughts continue. Because a gesture position affects a person's attitude, the longer a person holds the gesture, the longer the critical attitude will remain. This gesture is a signal that immediate action is required by the speaker, either by involving the listener in what he is saying or by ending the speech. A simple move, such as handing something to the listener to alter his pose, can cause a change in his attitude. This gesture is often mistaken as a signal of interest, but the supporting thumb tells the truth about the critical attitude (Figure 60).

Figure 60   *Having negative thoughts*

Chin-Stroking

The next time you have the opportunity to present an idea to a group of people, watch them carefully as you give your idea and you will notice something fascinating. Most, if not all the members of your audience will bring one hand up to their faces and begin to use evaluation gestures. As you come to the conclusion of your presentation and ask for the group to give opinions or suggestions about the idea, the evaluation gestures will cease. One hand will move to the chin and begin a chin-stroking gesture.

Figure 61 *Female version of chin-stroking*

Figure 62 *Making a decision*

This chin-stroking gesture is the signal that the listener is making a decision. When you have asked the listeners for a decision and their gestures have changed from evaluation to decision-making, the following movements will indicate whether their decision is negative or positive. A salesperson would be foolish to interrupt or to speak when a buyer begins the chin-stroking gesture after he has been asked for a decision to purchase. His best strategy would be a careful observation of the buyer's next gestures, which will indicate the decision he has reached. If, for example, the chin-stroking gesture is followed by crossed arms and legs and the buyer sits back in his chair, the salesperson has been non-verbally told, 'No'. He would be wise to review the main points of the presentation immediately before the buyer verbalizes his negative answer and the sale may be lost.

If the chin-stroking gesture is followed by the readiness gesture (Figure 97) the salesperson only needs to ask how the buyer would prefer to pay for the product and the buyer will proceed to make his purchase.

Variations of Decision-Making Gestures

Someone who wears glasses often follows evaluation clusters by removing them and putting one arm of the frame in his mouth instead of using the chin-stroking gesture when making a decision. A pipe-smoker will put his pipe in his mouth. When a person places an object such as a pen or a finger in his mouth after having been asked for a decision, it is a signal that he is unsure and reassurance is needed because the object in his mouth allows him to stall making an immediate decision. As it is bad manners to speak with your mouth full, the buyer feels justified in not giving an immediate decision.

Combination Hand-to-Face Clusters

Occasionally the boredom, evaluation and decision-making gestures come in combinations, each showing an element of the person's attitude.

Figure 63 shows the evaluation gesture moved to the chin, and the hand may also be stroking the chin. The person is evaluating the proposition, while making decisions at the same time. When the listener begins to lose interest in the speaker, the head begins to rest on the hand. Figure 64 shows evaluation with the head supported by the thumb as the listener becomes uninterested.

Figure 63   *Evaluation/decision cluster*

Figure 64   *Evaluation, decision, boredom cluster*

Head-Rubbing and Head-Slapping Gestures

An exaggerated version of the collar-pull gesture is the palm rubbing the back of the neck in what Calero called the 'pain-in-the-neck' gesture. A person who uses this when lying usually avoids your gaze and looks down. This gesture is also used as a signal of frustration or anger and, when this is the case, the hand slaps the back of the neck first and then begins to rub the neck. Let us assume, for example, that you asked a

Figure 65   *'Pain in the neck' gesture*

subordinate to complete a certain task for you and that the
subordinate had forgotten to do it within the time required.
When you ask him for the results, he non-verbally signals his
forgetfulness by slapping his head, either on the forehead or
the back of the neck, as if he were symbolically hitting himself. Although slapping of the head communicates forgetfulness, the person signals how he feels about you or the
situation by the position used when he slaps his hand on his
head, either the forehead or the neck. If he slaps his forehead
(Figure 66) he signals that he is not intimidated by your having mentioned his forgetfulness, but when he slaps the back
of his neck (Figure 65) he non-verbally tells you that you are

literally a 'pain-in-the-neck' for pointing out his error. Those who habitually rub the backs of their necks have a tendency to be negative or critical, whereas those who habitually rub their foreheads to non-verbalize an error tend to be more open, easy-going people.

Figure 66   *'Oh, no, not again!'*

Six

Arm Barriers

Folded-Arms Gestures

Hiding behind a barrier is a normal human response that we learn at an early age to protect ourselves. As children, we hid behind solid objects such as tables, chairs, furniture and mother's skirts whenever we found ourselves in a threatening situation. As we grew older, this hiding behavior became more sophisticated and by the age of about six, when it was unacceptable behavior to hide behind solid objects, we learned to fold our arms tightly across our chests whenever a threatening situation arose. During our teens, we learned to make this crossed-arms gesture a little less obvious by relaxing our arms a little and combining the gesture with crossed legs.

As we grow older, we develop the arm-crossing gesture to the point where it has become less obvious to others. By folding one or both arms across the chest, a barrier is formed that is, in essence, an attempt to block out the impending threat or undesirable circumstances. One thing is certain; when a person has a nervous, negative or defensive attitude, he will fold his arms firmly on his chest, a strong signal that he feels threatened.

Research conducted into the folded-arms position has shown some interesting results. A group of students was asked to attend a series of lectures and each student was instructed to keep his legs uncrossed, arms unfolded and to take a casual, relaxed sitting position. At the end of the lectures each student was tested on his retention and knowledge of the subject matter and his attitude toward the lecturer was recorded. A second group of students was put through the same process, but these students were instructed to keep their arms tightly folded across their chests throughout the lectures. The results showed that the group with the folded arms had learned and retained 38 percent less than the group who kept its arms unfolded. The second group also had a more critical opinion of the lectures and of the lecturer.

These tests reveal that, when the listener folds his arms, not only has he more negative thoughts about the speaker, but he is also paying less attention to what is being said. It is for this reason that training centers should have chairs with arms to allow the attendees to leave their arms uncrossed.

Many people claim that they habitually take the arms-folded position because it is comfortable. Any gesture will feel comfortable when you have the corresponding attitude; that is, if you have a negative, defensive or nervous attitude, the folded-arms position will feel good.

Remember that in non-verbal communication, the meaning of the message is also in the receiver, not only the sender. You may feel 'comfortable' with your arms crossed or your back and neck stiffened, but studies have shown that the reception of these gestures is negative.

Standard Arm-Cross Gesture

Both arms are folded together across the chest as an attempt to 'hide' from an unfavorable situation. There are many arm-folding positions, but this book will discuss the three most common ones. The standard arm-cross gesture (Figure 67) is a universal gesture signifying the same defensive or negative attitude almost everywhere. It is commonly seen when a person is among strangers in public meetings, lines, cafeterias, elevators or anywhere that people feel uncertain or insecure.

Figure 67 *Standard arm-cross*

During a recent lecture tour, I opened one particular meeting by deliberately defaming the character of several highly respected men who were well-known to the seminar audience and who were attending the conference. Immediately following the verbal attack, the members of the audience were asked to hold the positions and gestures they had taken. They were all quite amused when I pointed out that about 90 percent of them had taken the folded-arms position immediately after my verbal attack began. This clearly shows that most people will take an arms-folded position when they disagree with what they are hearing. Many public speakers have failed to communicate their message to the audience because they have not seen the folded-arms gestures of their listeners. Experienced speakers know that this gesture demonstrates the necessity of a good 'ice breaker' to move the audience into a more receptive posture that will alter their attitudes towards the speaker.

When you see the arm-cross gesture occur during a face-to-face encounter, it is reasonable to assume that you may have said something with which the other person disagrees, so it may be pointless continuing your line of argument even though the other person may be verbally agreeing with you. The fact is that the non-verbal medium does not lie—the verbal medium does. Your objective at this point should be to try to discover the cause of the arms-folded gesture and to move the person into a more receptive position. Remember: as long as the arms-folded gesture remains, the negative attitude will remain. The attitude causes the gestures to occur and prolonging the gesture forces the attitude to remain.

A simple but effective method of breaking the folded-arms position is to hand the person a pen, a book or something that forces him to unfold his arms to reach forward. This moves him into a more open posture and attitude. Asking the person to lean forward to look at a visual presentation can also be an effective means of opening the folded-arms position. Another useful method is to lean forward with your palms facing up and say, 'I can see you have a question, what would you like to know?' or, 'What do you think?' and then sit back to indicate that it is the other person's turn to speak. By leaving your palms visible you non-verbally tell the other person that you would like an open, honest answer. As a salesman, I would never proceed with the presentation of my product until I had uncovered the prospective buyer's reason for suddenly folding his arms. More often than not, I discovered that the buyer had a hidden objection that most other salespeople might never have discovered because they missed seeing the buyer's non-verbal signal that he was negative about some aspect of the sales presentation.

Reinforced Arm-Cross

If as well as the full arm-cross gesture the person has clenched fists, it indicates a hostile and defensive attitude. This cluster is often combined with clenched teeth and red face, in which case a verbal or physical attack may be imminent. A sub-missive palms-up approach is needed to discover what caused the hostile gestures if the reason is not already apparent. The person using this gesture cluster has an attacking attitude, as opposed to the person in Figure 67, who has taken a defending arm-cross position.

Figure 68 *Fists show a hostile attitude*

Arm-Gripping Gesture

You will notice that this arm-cross gesture is characterized by the hands tightly gripping the upper arms to reinforce the position and to stop any attempt to unfold the arms and expose the body. The arms can often be gripped so tightly that the fingers and knuckles turn white as the blood circulation is cut off. This arm-fold style is common to people sitting in doctors' and dentists' waiting rooms, or first-time air travelers who are waiting for the plane to take off. It shows a negative restrained attitude.

Figure 69 *A firm stand taken here*

In a lawyer's office the prosecutor may be seen using a fists-clenched arm-cross while the defense may have taken the arm-gripping position.

Status can influence arm-folding gestures. A superior type can make his superiority felt in the presence of persons he has just met by not folding his arms. Say, for example, that at a company social function, the general manager is introduced to several new employees whom he has not met. Having greeted them with a dominant handshake, he stands at the social distance from the new employees with his hands by his sides, behind his back in the superior palm-in-palm position (see Figure 42), or with one hand in his pocket. He rarely folds his arms to show the slightest hint of nervousness. Conversely, after shaking hands with the boss, the new employees take full or partial arm-fold gestures because of their apprehension about being in the presence of the company's top man. Both the general manager and the new employees feel comfortable with their respective gestures as each is signaling his status relative to the other. But what happens when the general manager meets a young, up-and-coming executive who is also a superior type and who may even feel that he is as important as the general manager? The likely outcome is that after the two give each other a dominant handshake, the young executive will make an arm-fold gesture with both thumbs pointing vertically upwards (Figure 70). This gesture is the defensive version of both arms being held horizontally in front of the body with both thumbs up to show that the user is 'cool', a gesture characterized by Henry Winkler who plays the Fonz in the television series *Happy Days*. The thumbs-up gesture is our way of showing that we have a self-confident attitude and the folded arms give a feeling of protection.

Salespeople need to analyze why a buyer may have made this gesture to know whether their approach is effective. If the thumbs-up gesture has come towards the end of the sales presentation and is combined with many other positive gestures used by the buyer, the salesperson can move comfort-

Figure 70 *Superior attitude shown*

Figure 71 *Holding hands with oneself*

ably into closing the sale and asking for the order. If, on the other hand, at the close of the sale the buyer moves into the fists-clenched arm-cross position (Figure 68) and has a poker face, the salesperson can be inviting disastrous consequences by attempting to ask for the order. Instead it is better if he quickly goes back to his sales presentation and asks more questions to try to discover the buyer's objection. In selling, if the buyer verbalizes, 'No', it can become difficult to change his decision. The ability to read body language allows you to see the negative decision before it is verbalized and gives you time to take an alternative course of action.

People who carry weapons or wear bulletproof vests rarely use defensive arm-fold gestures because their weapon or protective garment provides sufficient body protection. Police officers who wear guns, for example, rarely fold their arms unless they are standing guard and they normally use the fists-clenched position to show quite clearly that nobody is permitted to pass where they stand.

Partial Arm-Cross Barriers

The full arm-cross gesture is sometimes too obvious to use around others because it tells them that we are fearful. Occasionally we substitute a subtler version—the partial arm-cross, in which one arm swings across the body to hold or touch the other arm to form the barrier, as shown in Figure 72.

The partial arm barrier is often seen at meetings where a person may be a stranger to the group or is lacking in self-confidence. Another popular version of a partial arm barrier is holding hands with oneself (Figure 71), a gesture commonly used by people who stand before a crowd to receive an award or give a speech. Desmond Morris says that this gesture allows a person to relive the emotional security that he experi-

Figure 72 *Partial arm barrier*

enced as a child when his parent held his hand under fearful circumstances.

Disguised Arm-Cross Gestures

Disguised arm-cross gestures are highly sophisticated gestures used by people who are continually exposed to others. This group includes politicians, salespeople, television personalities and the like who do not want their audience to detect that they are unsure of themselves or nervous. Like all arm-cross gestures, one arm swings across in front of the body to grasp the other arm but instead of the arms folding, one hand touches a handbag, bracelet, watch, shirt cuff or other object on or near the other arm (Figure 73). Once again the barrier is formed and the secure feeling is achieved. When cufflinks were popular, men were often seen adjusting them as they crossed a room or dance floor where they were in full view of others. As cufflinks lost their popularity, a man would adjust the band on his watch, check the contents of his wal-

Figure 73 *Disguised nervousness*

let, clasp or rub his hands together, play with a button on his cuff or use any other gesture that would allow the arms to cross in front of the body. To the trained observer, however, these gestures are a dead giveaway because they achieve no real purpose except as an attempt to disguise nervousness. A good place to observe these gestures is anywhere that people walk past a group of onlookers, such as a young man who crosses the dance floor to ask an attractive young lady to dance with him or someone crossing an open room to receive a trophy.

Women are less obvious than men in their use of disguised arm-barrier gestures because they can grasp such things as handbags or purses when they become unsure of themselves (Figure 74). One of the most common versions of this is hold-

Figure 74 *Handbag used to form a barrier*

ing a glass of beer or wine with two hands. Did it ever occur to you that you need only one hand to hold a glass of wine? The use of two hands allows the nervous person to form an almost undetectable arm barrier. Having observed people using disguised arm-barrier signals on many occasions, we have found that these gestures are used by almost everyone. Many well-known figures in society also use disguised barrier signals in tense situations and are usually completely unaware that they are doing so.

Figure 75 *Flowers used to form a barrier*

Seven

Leg Barriers

Crossed-Leg Gestures

Like arm-barrier gestures, crossed legs are a signal that a negative or defensive attitude may exist. The purpose of crossing the arms on the chest was originally to defend the heart and upper body region and crossing the legs is an attempt to shield the genital area. Crossed arms also indicate a more negative attitude than do crossed legs, and the arms gesture is more obvious. Care should be taken when interpreting crossed-leg gestures with women as many have been taught that this is how to 'sit like a lady'. Unfortunately for them, however, the gesture can make them appear defensive.

There are two basic crossed-leg sitting positions, the standard leg cross and the leg lock in the shape of the number four.

The European Leg-Cross Position

One leg is crossed neatly over the other, usually the right over the left. This is the normal crossed-leg position used by European cultures and may be used to show a nervous, reserved or defensive attitude. However, this is usually a supportive gesture that occurs with other negative gestures and should not be interpreted in isolation or out of context. For example, people often sit like this during lectures or if they are on uncomfortable chairs for long periods. It is also common to see this gesture in cold weather. When the crossed-legs gesture is combined with crossed arms (Figure 77), the person has withdrawn from the conversation. A salesperson would be very foolish even to attempt to ask for a decision from a buyer when he has taken this pose, and the salesperson should ask probing questions to uncover his objection. This pose is popular among women in most countries, particularly to show their displeasure with a husband or boyfriend.

Figure 76 *The standard leg cross*

Figure 77 *Woman showing displeasure*

The Leg-Lock Position

This leg cross indicates that an argumentative or competitive attitude exists. It is the sitting position used by many American males who have a competitive nature. This being the case, it is difficult to interpret the attitude of an American during a conversation, but it is quite obvious when this gesture is used by a British citizen.

I recently addressed a series of meetings where the audience comprised about 100 managers and 500 salespeople. A highly controversial issue was being discussed—the treatment of salespeople by corporations. A salesman who was well-known to the audience and who had a reputation as a stirrer was asked to address the group. As he took the stage, the managers, almost without exception, took the defensive pose shown in Figure 77, which showed that they felt threatened by what they thought the salesman was going to say. Their fears were well-founded. The salesman raged about the poor quality of management in most corporations in that industry and said he felt that this was a contributing factor to the industry's staffing problems. Throughout his speech the salespeople in the audience were leaning forward showing interest, many using evaluation gestures, but the managers held their defensive positions. The salesman then changed his address to discuss what he believed the manager's role should be in relation to the salespeople. Almost as if they were players in an orchestra who had been given a command by the orchestra leader, the managers shifted to the competitive/argumentative position (Figure 78). It was obvious that they were mentally debating the salesman's point of view and many later confirmed that this had been the case. I noticed, however, that several managers had not taken this pose. After the meeting I asked them why, and, although most said they had also disagreed with the salesman's views, they were unable to sit in the leg-lock position for such reasons as obesity and arthritis.

Figure 78 *The American position*

In a selling situation it would be unwise to attempt to close the sale and ask for the order when the buyer takes this position. The salesperson would need to use an open appeal, leaning forward with palms up and saying, 'I can see you have some ideas on this. I'd be interested in your opinion', and then sit back to signify that it is the buyer's turn to speak. This gives the buyer an opportunity to tell you his opinion. Women wearing trousers or jeans are also observed sitting in the figure 4 position on occasions.

Leg Clamp and the Leg Lock

The person who has a hard and fast attitude in an argument or debate will often lock the leg into place with one or both hands, using them as a clamp. This is a sign of the tough-minded, stubborn individual who may need a special approach to break through his resistance.

Figure 79 *Arms lock the leg in place*

Standing Leg-Cross Gestures

The next time you attend a meeting or function, you will notice small groups of people all standing with their arms and legs crossed (Figure 80). Observation will also reveal that they are standing at a greater distance from each other than the customary one, and that, if they are wearing coats or jackets,

Figure 80 *Defensive standing position*

they are usually buttoned. If you were to question these people, you would find that one or all of them are strangers to the others in the group. This is how most people stand when they are among people whom they do not know well.

Now you notice another small group in which the people are standing with arms unfolded, palms exposed, coats unbuttoned, relaxed appearance, leaning on one foot with the other pointing towards other members of the group and moving in and out of each other's intimate zones. Close investigation reveals that these people are friends or are known personally to each other. Interestingly, the people using the closed arms and legs stance may have relaxed facial expressions and conversation that sounds free and easy, but the folded arms and legs tell us that they are not relaxed or confident.

The next time you join a group of people who are standing in the open friendly stance but among whom you know no one, stand with your arms and legs tightly crossed. One by one the other group members will cross their arms and legs and remain in that position until you leave them. Then walk away and watch how, one by one, the members of the group assume their original open pose once again!

The 'Opening-Up' Procedure

As people begin to feel comfortable in a group and get to know others in it, they move through an unwritten code of movements taking them from the defensive crossed arms and legs position to the relaxed open position.

Stage 1: Defensive position, arms and legs crossed (Figure 81).

Stage 2: Legs uncrossed and feet placed together in a neutral position.

Stage 3: The arm folded on top in the arm-cross comes out and the palm is flashed when speaking but is not tucked back into the arm-cross position. It holds the outside of the other arm.

Stage 4: Arms unfold and one arm gesticulates or may be placed on the hip or in the pocket.

Stage 5: One person leans back on one leg and pushes the other forward to point at the person whom he finds the most interesting (Figure 82).

Alcohol can speed up this process or eliminate some of the stages.

Figure 81   *Closed body and closed attitude*

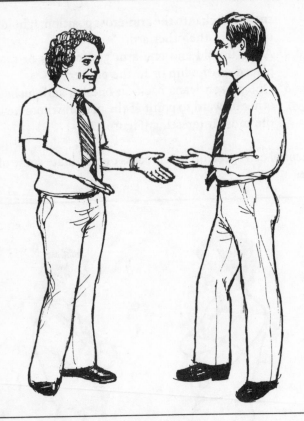

Figure 82 *Open body and open attitude*

Defensive or Cold?

Many people claim that they are not defensive but cross their arms or legs because they feel cold. This is often a cover-up and it is interesting to note the difference between a defensive stance and the way a person stands when he or she feels cold. First of all, when someone wants to warm his hands he normally thrusts them into the armpits rather than tucking them under the elbows, as is the case with a defensive arm-cross. Secondly, when a person feels cold he may fold his arms in a type of body hug and when the legs are crossed they are usually straight, stiff and pressed hard against each other (Figure 83), as opposed to the more relaxed leg posture of the defensive stance or position.

People who habitually take a crossed arms or legs position prefer to say that they are cold or comfortable rather than to admit that they could be nervous, shy or defensive.

Figure 83 *This woman is probably cold, but she may wish to go to the bathroom*

The Ankle-Lock Gesture

Crossing or folding the arms or legs suggests that a negative or defensive attitude exists, and this is also the case with the ankle-lock gesture. The male version of the ankle lock is often combined with clenched fists resting on the knees or with the hands tightly gripping the arms of the chair (Figure 84). The female version varies slightly; the knees are held together, the feet may be to one side and the hands rest side by side or one on top of the other resting on the upper legs (Figure 85).

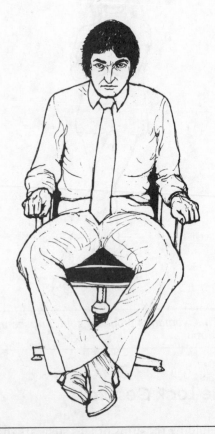

Figure 84 *Male version of the ankle lock*

Figure 85   *Female version of the ankle lock*

During more than a decade of interviewing and selling to people, our observation has revealed that, when the interviewee locks his ankles, he is mentally 'biting his lip'. The gesture is one of holding back a negative attitude, emotion, nervousness or fear. For example, a lawyer friend of mine told me that he had often noticed that, just prior to a court hearing, the people who were involved in the case nearly always sat with their ankles tightly locked together. He also found that they had been waiting to say something or had been trying to control their emotional state.

When interviewing prospective employees, we noted that most job applicants locked their ankles at some point during the interview, indicating that they were holding back an emotion or attitude. In the initial stages of our research with this gesture, we found that asking questions about the job applicant's feelings was often unsuccessful in unlocking his ankles and thus his mind. We soon discovered, however, that if the interviewer walked around to the job applicant's side of the desk and sat beside him, removing the desk barrier, the job applicant's ankles would often unlock and the conversation took on an open, more personal atmosphere.

We were recently advising a company on the effective use of the telephone to contact customers when we met a young man who had the unenviable job of calling customers who had not paid their accounts. We watched him make a number of calls and, although he sounded relaxed, we noticed that his ankles were locked together beneath his chair. I asked, 'How do you enjoy this job?' He replied, 'Fine! It's a lot of fun.' This verbal statement was, however, inconsistent with his nonverbal signals, although he did sound quite convincing. 'Are you sure?' I asked. He paused for a moment, unlocked his ankles, turned towards me with open palms and said, 'Well, actually, it drives me crazy!' He then told me that he had received several calls from customers who had been rude to him and he had been holding back his feelings so as not to transmit them to the other customers. Interestingly, we have noticed that salespeople who do not enjoy using the telephone sit in the locked ankles position.

Leaders in the field of negotiating techniques, Nierenberg and Calero, found that whenever one party locked his ankles during a negotiation it often meant that he was holding back a valuable concession. They found that, by using questioning techniques, they could often encourage him to unlock his ankles and reveal the concession.

There are always people who claim that they habitually sit in the ankle-lock position, or for that matter, any of the negative arm and leg clusters, because they feel comfortable. If you are one of these people, remember that any arm or leg position will feel comfortable when you have a defensive, negative or reserved attitude. Considering that a negative gesture can increase or prolong a negative attitude, and that other people interpret you as being defensive or negative, you would be well advised to practice using positive and open gestures to improve your self-confidence and relationships with others.

Women who were teenagers during the mini-skirt era crossed their legs and ankles for obvious, necessary reasons. Through habit, many of these women still sit in this position, which may make others misinterpret them; people may react toward these women with caution. It is important to take female fashion trends into consideration, particularly how these may affect the woman's leg positions, before jumping to conclusions.

The Foot Lock

This gesture is almost exclusively used by women. The top of one foot locks around the other leg to reinforce a defensive attitude and, when this gesture appears, you can be sure that the woman has become a mental recluse or has retreated like a tortoise into her shell. A warm, friendly, low-key approach is needed if you eventually hope to open this clam. This position is common in shy or timid women.

I recall an interview in which a new salesman was trying to sell insurance to a young married couple. The sale was unsuccessful and the new salesman could not understand why he had lost it, because he had followed the sales track perfectly. I pointed out that he had failed to notice that the woman was sitting with a tight foot-lock position throughout the interview. Had the salesman understood the significance of this gesture, he could have involved her in the sales presentation, and might have achieved a better result.

Figure 86   *Standing foot-lock position*

Figure 87   *Seated foot-lock position*

Eight

Other Popular Gestures and Actions

Straddling a Chair

Centuries ago, men used shields to protect themselves from the spears and clubs of the enemy, and today, civilized man uses whatever he has at his disposal to symbolize this same protective behavior when he is under physical or verbal attack. This includes standing behind a gate, doorway, fence, desk, the open door of his motor vehicle and straddling a chair (Figure 88). The back of the chair provides a shield to protect his body and can transform him into an aggressive, dominant warrior. Most chair straddlers are dominant individuals who will try to take control of other people or groups when they become bored with the conversation, and the back of the chair serves as good protection from any 'attack' by other members of the group. He is often discreet and can slip into the straddle position almost unnoticed.

The easiest way to disarm the straddler is to stand or sit behind him, making him feel vulnerable to attack and forcing him to change his position, becoming less aggressive. This can work well in groups because the straddler will have his back exposed; this forces him to change position.

But how do you handle a one-to-one confrontation with a straddler on a swivel chair? It is pointless to try to reason with

Figure 88 *The straddler*

him, particularly when he is on a swiveling merry-go-round, so the best defense is non-verbal attack. Conduct your conversation standing above and looking down upon the straddler and move within his personal territory. This is very disconcerting to him and he may even fall backwards off his chair in an attempt to avoid being forced to change position.

If you have a straddler coming to visit you and his aggressive attitude annoys you, be sure to seat him on a fixed chair that has arms to stop him from taking his favorite position.

Picking Imaginary Lint

When a person disapproves of the opinions or attitudes of others but feels constrained in giving his point of view, the non-verbal gestures that occur are known as displacement gestures, that is, they result from a withheld opinion. Picking imaginary pieces of lint from the clothing is one such gesture. The lint-picker usually looks away from the other people towards the floor while performing this minor, irrelevant action. This is one of the most common signals of disapproval and when the listener continually picks imaginary pieces of lint off his clothing it is a good indication that he does not like what is being said, even though he may be verbally agreeing with everything.

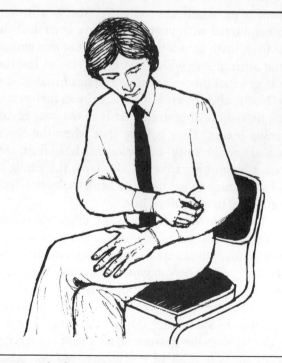

Figure 89   *The lint-picker*

Open your palms and say, 'Well, what do you think?' or, 'I can see you have some thoughts on this. Would you mind telling me what they are?' Sit back, arms apart, palms visible, and wait for the answer. If the person says he is in agreement with you but continues to pick the imaginary lint, you may need to take an even more direct approach to discover his hidden objection.

Head Gestures

This book would not be complete without a discussion of the basic head movements, the two most widely used being the head nod and the head shake. The head nod is a positive gesture used in most cultures to signify, 'Yes', or affirmation. Research conducted with people who have been deaf, dumb and blind from birth shows that they also use this gesture to signify the affirmative, which has given rise to the theory that this may be an inborn gesture. The head shake, usually meaning 'No', is also claimed by some to be an inborn action; however, others have theorized that it is the first gesture a human being learns. They believe that when the newborn baby has had enough milk, he shakes his head from side to side to reject his mother's breast. Similarly, the young child who has had enough to eat uses the head shake to reject his parent's attempt to spoonfeed him.

One of the easiest ways to uncover a disguised objection when dealing with others is to watch if the person uses the head shake gesture while verbalizing his agreement with you. Take, for example, the person who verbalizes, 'Yes, I can see your point of view', or, 'I really enjoy working here', or, 'We'll definitely do business after Christmas', while shaking his head from side to side. Even though this may sound convincing, the head shake gesture signals that a negative attitude exists and you would be well advised to reject what the person has said and to question him further.

Basic Head Positions

There are three basic head positions. The first is with the head up (Figure 90) and is the position taken by the person who has a neutral attitude about what he is hearing. The head usually remains still and may occasionally give small nods. Hand-to-cheek evaluation gestures are often used with this position.

Figure 90   *Neutral head position*   **Figure 91**   *Interested position*

When the head tilts to one side it shows that interest has developed (Figure 91). Charles Darwin was one of the first to note that humans, as well as animals, tilt their heads to one side when they become interested in something. If you are giving a sales presentation or delivering a speech, always make a point of looking for this gesture among your audience. When you see them tilt their heads and lean forward using hand-to-chin evaluation gestures, you are getting the point across. Women use this head position to show interest in an attractive male. When others are speaking to you, all you need do is use the head-tilted position and head nods to make the listener feel warm towards you.

When the head is down, it signals that the attitude is negative and even judgmental (Figure 92). Critical evaluation clusters are normally made with the head down and, unless you can get the person's head up or tilted, you may have a communication problem. As a public speaker, you will often be confronted by an audience whose members are all seated with head down and arms folded on the chest. Professional speakers and trainers usually do something that involves audience participation before they begin their address. This is intended to get the audience's heads up and to get them involved. If the speaker's ploy is successful, the audience's next head position will be the head tilted.

Figure 92 *Disapproval position*

Both Hands Behind Head

This gesture is typical of such professionals as accountants, lawyers, sales managers, bank managers or people who are feeling confident, dominant, or superior about something. If we could read the person's mind, he would be saying something like, 'I have all the answers' or, 'Maybe one day you'll be as smart as I am', or even 'Everything's under control'. It is also a gesture used by the 'know-it-all' individual and many people find it irritating when someone does it to them. Lawyers habitually use this with their peers as a non-verbal demonstration of how knowledgeable they are. It can also be used as a territorial sign to show that the person has staked a claim to that particular area. The man in Figure 93 has also taken a leg-lock position in the shape of the number four which shows that he not only feels superior but is also likely to want to argue.

Figure 93 *'Maybe someday you'll be as smart as I am.'*

There are several ways to handle this gesture, depending on the circumstances in which it occurs. If you want to discover the reason for the person's superior attitude, lean forward with palms up and say, 'I can see that you know about this. Would you care to comment?' Then sit back, palms still visible, and wait for an answer. Another method is to force the man to change his position, which will in turn change his attitude. This can be accomplished by placing something just out of his reach and asking, 'Have you seen this?', forcing him to lean forward. Copying the gesture is another good way to handle it. If you want to show that you agree with the other person, all you need do is copy his gestures.

On the other hand, if the person using the hands-behind-head gesture is reprimanding you, you will non-verbally intimidate him by copying this gesture. For example, two lawyers will use the gesture in each other's presence (Figure 94) to show equality and agreement, but the mischievous school-boy would infuriate the school principal if he used it in his office.

Figure 94 *'I'm just as smart as you are!'*

The origin of this gesture is uncertain, but it is likely that the hands are used as an imaginary armchair in which the person lies back and relaxes.

Research into this gesture showed that in one particular insurance company, twenty-seven out of thirty sales managers used it regularly in the presence of their salespeople or subordinates but seldom in the presence of their superiors. When they were with their superiors, the same managers used submissive and defensive gesture clusters.

Aggressive and Readiness Gestures

Which gesture is used in the following situations: the young child arguing with his parent, the athlete waiting for his event to begin and the boxer in the dressing room waiting for the bout to start?

In each instance, the individual is seen standing with the hands-on-hips pose, for this is one of the most common gestures used by man to communicate an aggressive attitude. Some observers have labeled this gesture 'readiness' which in the right context is correct, but the basic meaning is aggression. It has also been called the achiever stance, related to the goal-directed individual who uses this position when he is ready to tackle his objectives. These observations are correct because in both cases the person is ready to take action about something, but it still remains an aggressive, forward-moving gesture. Men often use this gesture in the presence of women to show an aggressive, dominant male attitude.

It is interesting to note that birds fluff their feathers to make themselves appear bigger when they are fighting or courting; humans use the hands-on-hips gesture for the same purpose, that is, to make themselves appear bigger. Males will use it as a non-verbal challenge to other males who enter their territory.

It is also important to consider the circumstances and gestures immediately preceding the hands-on-hips pose to make a correct assessment of the person's attitude. Several other gestures can further support your conclusion. For example, is the coat open and pushed back on to the hips, or is it buttoned when the aggressive pose is taken? Closed-coat readiness shows aggressive frustration, whereas coat open and pushed back (Figure 95) is a directly aggressive pose because the person is openly exposing his heart and throat in a non-verbal display of fearlessness. This position can be even further reinforced by placing the feet evenly apart on the ground or by adding clenched fists to the gesture cluster.

Figure 95   *Ready for action*

The aggressive-readiness clusters are used by professional models to give the impression that their clothing is for the modern, aggressive, forward-thinking woman. Occasionally the gesture may be done with only one hand on the hip and the other displaying another gesture (Figure 96). Critical evaluation gestures are often seen with the hands-on-hips pose.

Figure 96   *Hands-on-hips gesture used to make clothing seem more appealing*

Seated Readiness

One of the most valuable gestures that a negotiator can learn to recognize is seated readiness. In the selling situation, for example, if the potential buyer were to take this gesture at the end of the sales presentation and the interview had progressed successfully up to that point, the salesperson could ask for the order and expect to get it. Video replays of insurance salespeople interviewing potential buyers revealed that, whenever the seated-readiness gesture followed the chin-stroking gesture (decision-making), the client bought the policy. In contrast to this, if, during the close of the sale, the client took the arms-crossed position immediately following the chin-stroking gesture, the sale was usually unsuccessful. Unfortunately, most sales courses teach salespeople always to ask for the order with little regard for the client's body position and gestures. Learning to recognize such gestures as readiness not only helps make more sales but helps to keep many more people in the selling profession. The seated-readiness gesture is also taken by the angry person who is ready for something else—to throw you out. The preceding gesture clusters give the correct assessment of the person's intentions.

Figure 97   *Ready to proceed*

The Starter's Position

The readiness gestures that signal a desire to end a conversation or encounter are leaning forward with both hands on both knees (Figure 98), or leaning forward with both hands gripping the chair (Figure 99). Should either of these occur during a conversation it could be wise for you to take the lead and terminate it. This allows you to maintain a psychological advantage and to keep the control.

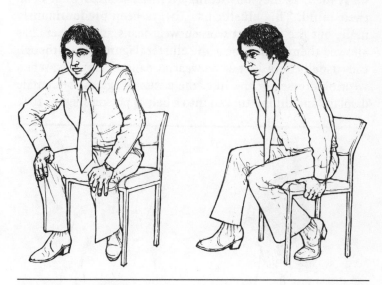

Figure 98 *Readiness to end an encounter or a conversation: hands on knees*

Figure 99 *On your mark, get set: leaning forward gripping the chair*

Sexual Aggressiveness

Thumbs tucked into the belt or the tops of the pockets is the gesture display used to show a sexually aggressive attitude. It is one of the most common gestures used in television Westerns to show viewers the virility of their favorite gunslinger (Figure 100). The arms take the readiness position and the hands serve as central indicators, highlighting the genital region. Men use this gesture to stake their territory or to show other men that they are unafraid. When it is used in the presence of females, the gesture can be interpreted as, 'I am virile, I can dominate you'.

This gesture, combined with expanded pupils and one foot pointing toward a female, is easily decoded by most women. It is this gesture that non-verbally gives the game away for most men, as they unwittingly tell the woman what is on their mind. This cluster has always been predominantly male, but the fact that women wear jeans and trousers has allowed them to use the same cluster (Figure 101), although they usually only do it when wearing pants or trousers. When wearing dresses or the like, the sexually aggressive female displays one thumb tucked into a belt or pocket (Figure 101).

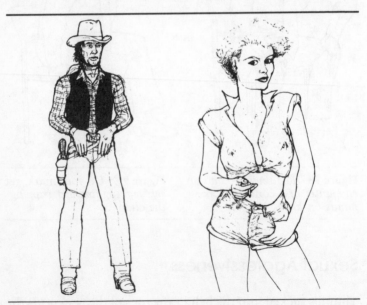

Figure 100   *The cowboy stance*   **Figure 101**   *The sexually aggressive female*

Male-Male Aggression

Figure 102 shows two men sizing each other up, using the characteristic hands-on-hips and thumbs-in-belt gestures. Considering that they are both turned at an angle away from each other and the lower halves of their bodies are relaxed, it would be reasonable to assume that these two males are unconsciously evaluating each other and that an attack is unlikely. Their conversation may be casual or friendly but a completely relaxed atmosphere will not exist until their hands-on-hips gestures cease and open palm gestures are used.

Figure 102 *Sizing each other up*

If these two men had been directly facing each other with their feet planted firmly on the ground, a fight would be likely to occur (Figure 103).

Figure 103   *Trouble brewing*

Nine

Eye Signals

Throughout history, we have been preoccupied with the eye and its effect on human behavior. We have all used such phrases as 'She looked daggers at him', 'She has big baby eyes', 'He has shifty eyes', 'She has inviting eyes', 'He had that gleam in his eye' or 'He gave me the Evil Eye'. When we use these phrases we unwittingly refer to the size of the person's pupils and to his or her gaze behavior. In his book *The Tell-Tale Eye*, Hess says that the eyes may well give the most revealing and accurate of all human communication signals because they are a focal point on the body and the pupils work independently.

In given light conditions, the pupils will dilate or contract as the person's attitude and mood change from positive to negative and vice versa. When someone becomes excited, his pupils can dilate up to four times their normal size. Conversely, an angry, negative mood causes the pupils to contract to what are commonly known as 'beady little eyes' or 'snake eyes'. The eyes are used a lot in courtship; women use eye make-up to emphasize their eye display. If a woman loves a man, she will dilate her pupils at him and he will decode this signal correctly, without knowing he does so. For this reason, romantic encounters are often arranged in dimly lit places that cause the pupils to dilate.

Young lovers who look deeply into each other's eyes unknowingly look for pupil dilation; each becomes excited by the dilation of the other's pupils. Research has shown that

Figure 104 *'Beady' little eyes*   **Figure 105** *Bedroom eyes*

when pornographic films showing men and women in sexual positions are shown to men, their pupils can dilate to almost three times the normal size. When the same films are shown to women their pupil dilation is even greater than that recorded by the men, which raises some doubt about the statement that women are less stimulated by pornography than men.

Young babies and children have larger pupils than adults and their pupils constantly dilate when adults are present in an attempt to look as appealing as possible and thus receive constant attention.

Tests conducted with expert card players show that fewer games were won by the experts when their opponents wore dark glasses. For example, if an opponent were dealt four aces in a game of poker, his rapid pupil dilation would be unconsciously detected by the expert, who would get a feeling that he should not bet on the next hand. Dark glasses worn by the opponents eliminated pupil signals and as a result the experts won fewer games than usual.

Pupil watching was used by the ancient Chinese gem traders who watched for the pupil dilation of their buyers when negotiating prices. Centuries ago, prostitutes put drops of belladonna in their eyes to dilate their pupils and to make themselves appear more desirable. The late Aristotle Onassis was noted for wearing dark glasses when negotiating business deals so that his eyes would not reveal his thoughts.

An old cliché says, 'Look a person in the eye when you talk to him.' When you are communicating or negotiating with others, practice 'looking them in the pupil' and let the pupils tell you their real feelings.

Gaze Behavior

It is only when you see 'eye to eye' with another person that a real basis for communication can be established. While some people can make us feel quite comfortable when they converse with us, others can make us feel ill-at-ease and some seem untrustworthy. This has to do primarily with the length of time that they look at us or hold our gaze as they speak. When a person is being dishonest or holding back information, his eyes meet ours less than one-third of the time. When a person's gaze meets yours for more than two-thirds of the time, it can mean one of two things; first, he or she finds you very interesting or appealing, in which case the gaze will be associated with dilated pupils; secondly, he or she is hostile towards you and may be issuing a non-verbal challenge, in which case the pupils will become constricted. Argyle reported that he found that when person A likes person B, he will look at him a lot. This causes B to think that A likes him, so B will like A in return. In other words, to build a good rapport with another person, your gaze should meet his about 60 to 70 percent of the time. This will also make him begin to like you. It is not surprising, therefore, that the nervous, timid person who meets your gaze less than one-third of the time is rarely trusted. In negotiation, dark tinted glasses should be avoided at all times as they make others feel that you are staring at them.

Like most body language and gestures, the length of time that one person gazes at another is culturally determined. Southern Europeans have a high frequency of gaze that may be offensive to others and the Japanese gaze at the neck rather than at the face when conversing. Always be sure to consider cultural circumstances before jumping to conclusions.

Not only is the length of the gaze significant; just as important is the geographical area of the person's face and body at which you direct your gaze, as this also affects the outcome of a negotiation. These signals are transmitted and received non-verbally and are accurately interpreted by the receiver.

It takes about thirty days of conscious practice before the following eye techniques can be effectively used to improve your communication skills.

The Business Gaze

When having discussions on a business level, imagine that there is a triangle on the other person's forehead. By keeping your gaze directed at this area, you create a serious atmosphere and the other person senses that you mean business. Provided that your gaze does not drop below the level of the other person's eyes, you are able to maintain control of the interaction.

Figure 106 *The business gaze*

The Social Gaze

When the gaze drops below the other person's eye level, a social atmosphere develops. Experiments in gazing reveal that during social encounters the gazer's eyes also look in a triangular area on the other person's face, in this case between the eyes and the mouth.

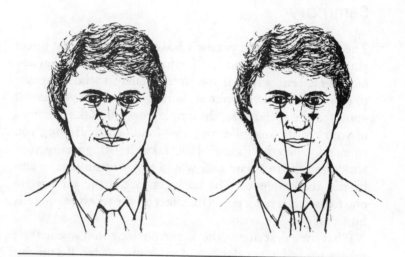

Figure 107 *The social gaze*   **Figure 108** *The intimate gaze*

The Intimate Gaze

The gaze is across the eyes and below the chin to other parts of the person's body. In close encounters it is the triangular area between the eyes and the chest or breasts and for distant gazing from the eyes to the crotch. Men and women use this gaze to show interest in each other and those who are interested will return the gaze.

Sideways Glance

The sideways glance is used to communicate either interest or hostility. When it is combined with slightly raised eyebrows or a smile, it communicates interest and is frequently used as a courtship signal. If it is combined with down-turned eyebrows, furrowed brow or the corners of the mouth down-turned, it signals a suspicious, hostile or critical attitude.

Summary

The area of the other person's body upon which you direct your gaze can have a powerful effect on the outcome of any face-to-face encounter. If you were a manager who was going to reprimand a lazy employee, which gaze would you use? If you used the social gaze, the employee would take less heed of your words, regardless of how loud or threatening you sounded. The social gaze would take the sting out of your words and the intimate gaze would either intimidate or embarrass the employee. The business gaze is the appropriate one to use, as it has a powerful effect on the receiver and tells him that you are serious.

What men describe as the 'come-on' look that women use relates to a sideways glance and an intimate gaze. If a man or woman wants to play hard to get, he or she needs only avoid using the intimate gaze and instead use the social gaze. To use the business gaze during courting would cause a man or woman to be labeled as cold or unfriendly. The point is that when you use the intimate gaze on a potential sex partner, you give the game away. Women are expert at sending and receiving this type of gaze but unfortunately, most men are not. Men are usually obvious when they use the intimate gaze and they are generally unaware of having been given an intimate gaze, much to the frustration of the woman who has transmitted it.

Eye-Block Gesture

Some of the most irritating people with whom we deal are those who use the eye-block gesture as they speak. This gesture occurs unconsciously and is an attempt by the person to block you from his sight because he has become bored or uninterested in you or feels that he is superior to you. Compared to the normal rate of six to eight blinks per minute during conversation, the eyelids close and remain closed for a second or longer as the person momentarily wipes you from his mind. The ultimate blockout is to leave the eyes closed and to fall asleep, but this rarely happens during one-to-one encounters.

If a person feels superior to you, the eye-block gesture is combined with the head tilted backwards to give you a long look, commonly known as 'looking down one's nose'. When you see an eye-block gesture during a conversation, it is a signal that the approach you are using may be causing a negative reaction and that a new tack is needed if effective communication is to take place (Figure 109).

Figure 109 *Shutting everyone out*

Controlling a Person's Gaze

It is worth discussing at this point how to control a person's gaze when you are giving him a visual presentation using books, charts, graphs and so on. Research shows that of the

Figures 110 & 111 *Using the pen to keep control of a person's gaze*

information relayed to a person's brain, 87 percent comes via the eyes, 9 percent via the ears, and 4 percent via the other senses. If, for example, the person is looking at your visual aid as you are speaking, he will absorb as little as 9 percent of your message if the message is *not* directly related to what he sees. If the message *is* related to the visual aid, he will absorb only 25 to 30 percent of your message if he is looking at the visual aid. To maintain maximum control of his gaze, use a pen or pointer to point to the visual aid and at the same time verbalize what he sees (Figure 110). Next, lift the pen from the visual aid and hold it between his eyes and your own eyes (Figure 111). This has the magnetic effect of lifting his head so that he is looking at your eyes and now he sees and hears what you are saying, thus achieving maximum absorption of your message. Be sure that the palm of your other hand is visible when you are speaking.

Ten

Courtship Gestures and Signals

I have a friend named Graham who has developed an art that most males would love to acquire. Whenever he attends a social function he can quickly 'psych out' the available women, make his choice and, in almost record-breaking time (sometimes as little as ten minutes), he may be seen heading towards the exit with the woman, escorting her to his car and driving back to his apartment. I have even seen him return to the party within an hour and repeat this amazing process two or three times in the same evening. He seems to have built-in radar for finding the right girl at the right time and getting her to go with him. Many people wonder: what is the key to his success? Perhaps you know someone like Graham and have asked yourself the same question.

Research on animal courtship behavior conducted by zoologists and behavioral scientists reveals that male and female animals use a series of intricate courtship gestures, some quite obvious and others extremely subtle, and that most are done subconsciously. In the animal world, courtship behavior in each species follows specific and predetermined patterns. For example, in several species of bird, the male struts around the female giving a vocal display, puffing up his feathers and performing many intricate body movements to gain her attention, while the female appears to display little or no interest. This ritual is similar to that performed by the human animal when courtship begins. Graham's technique was to display male courtship gestures to the prospective females and those who were interested would respond with the appropriate female courtship signals, giving Graham the non-verbal green light to proceed with a more intimate approach.

The success that people have in sexual encounters with members of the opposite sex is directly related to their ability to send courtship signals and to recognize those being sent back. Women are aware of the courtship gestures, as they are aware of most other body gestures, but men are far less perceptive, often being totally blind to them.

It was interesting to note that women described Graham as 'sexy', 'masculine', and 'someone who makes you feel feminine'; their reactions to his constant array of courtship signals. Men, on the other hand, described him as 'aggressive', 'insincere', and 'arrogant'; their reaction to the aggressive competition that Graham represented. Consequently, he had very few male friends, and the reasons for this should be obvious—no male likes a rival for the attentions of his female.

'What gestures and body movements do people use to communicate desire for involvement?' is frequently asked. We will now list the signals used by both sexes to attract potential sexual partners. You will note that more space is devoted to female courtship signals than to male signals; this is because women have a greater range of courtship signals than men.

While some courtship signals are studied and deliberate, others are given completely unconsciously. How we learn these signals is difficult to explain and a popular theory is that they may be inborn.

Dr. Albert Scheflen, in his article 'Quasi-courtship behavior in psychotherapy', noted that when a person enters the company of a member of the opposite sex, certain physiological changes take place. He found that high muscle tone became evident in preparation for a possible sexual encounter, 'bagging' around the face and eyes decreased, body sagging disappeared, the chest protruded, the stomach was automatically pulled in, pot-bellied slumping disappeared, the body assumed an erect posture and the person appeared to become more youthful in appearance. The ideal place to observe these changes is on a beach when a man and woman approach each other from a distance. The changes take place when the man and woman are close enough to meet each other's gaze and continue until after they have passed each other, at which time the original posture returns (Figures 112 to 114).

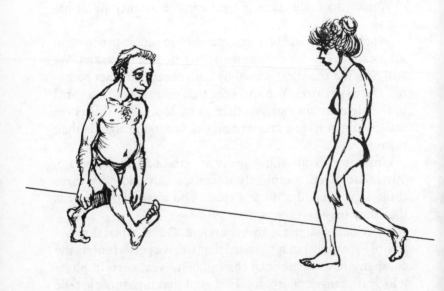

Figure 112   *Man and woman approaching on a beach*

Figure 113   *They see each other*

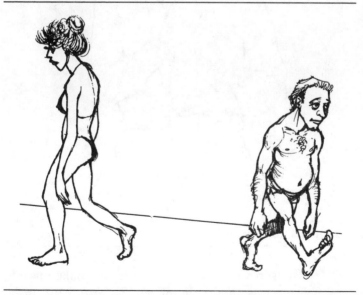

Figure 114   *They pass each other*

Male Courtship Gestures

Like most animal species, the human male displays preening behavior as the female approaches. In addition to the automatic physiological reactions already mentioned, he will reach for his throat and straighten his tie. If he is not wearing a tie, he may smooth his collar or brush imaginary dust from his shoulder and rearrange cufflinks, shirt, coat and other clothing. He may also preen himself by smoothing his hair.

Figure 115 *Male preening gesture*

The most aggressive sexual display he can make towards the female is the aggressive thumbs-in-belt gesture that highlights his genital region (see Figure 100). He may also turn his body towards her and point his foot at her. He uses the intimate gaze (Figure 108) and holds her gaze for a split second longer than normal. If he is really interested his pupils will be dilated. He often stands with his hands on hips (Figure 95) to accentuate his physical size and show his readiness to be involved with the female. When seated or leaning against a wall, he may also spread his legs to give a crotch display.

When it comes to courtship rituals, most men are about as effective as someone standing in a river trying to catch fish by hitting them on the head with a big stick. Women, as we shall see, have more lures and fishing skills to land their fish than any male could ever hope to acquire.

Female Courtship Gestures and Signals

Women use most of the same basic preening gestures as men, including touching the hair, smoothing the clothing, one or both hands on hips, foot and body pointing towards the male, extended intimate gaze and increasing eye contact. They also adopt the thumbs-in-belt gesture which, although it is a male aggression gesture, is used with feminine subtlety; only one thumb tucked into a belt or protruding from a handbag or pocket is displayed.

Excited interest also causes pupil dilation and a flushed appearance in the cheeks. Other female courtship signals follow.

The Head Toss

The head is flicked to toss the hair back over the shoulders or away from the face. Even women with short hair may use this gesture.

Exposed Wrists

An interested female will gradually expose the smooth soft skin of her wrists to the potential male partner. The wrist area has long been considered one of the highly erotic areas of the body. The palms are also made visible to the male while she is speaking. Women who smoke cigarettes find this tantalizing wrist/palm exposure quite simple to perform while smoking. The exposed wrist and head-toss gestures are often mimicked by homosexual males who want to take on a feminine appearance.

Figure 116   *Courtship cluster used to sell cigarettes*

Open Legs

The legs are opened wider than they would normally have been if the male had not arrived on the scene. This occurs whether the woman is sitting or standing and contrasts with the sexually defensive female who keeps her legs crossed and together at all times.

Rolling Hips

The hips have an accentuated roll when walking to highlight the pelvic region.

Figure 117   *Female preening gestures*

Some of the more subtle female courtship gestures that follow have been used for centuries in advertising to sell goods and services.

Sideways Glance

With partially dropped eyelids, the woman holds the man's gaze just long enough for him to notice, then she quickly looks away. This has the tantalizing feeling of peeping and being peeped at and can light the fires of most normal men.

Mouth Slightly Open, Wet Lips

Dr. Desmond Morris describes this as 'self-mimicry' as it is intended to symbolize the female genital region. The lips can be made to appear wet either by the use of saliva or cosmetics. Both give the woman the appearance of sexual invitation.

Lipstick

When a woman becomes sexually aroused, her lips, breasts and genitals become larger and redder as they fill with blood. The use of lipstick is a technique thousands of years old that is intended to mimic the reddened genitals of the sexually aroused female.

Fondling a Cylindrical Object

Fondling cigarettes, the stem of a wine glass, a finger or any long, thin object is an unconscious indication of what may be in the mind.

Sideways Glance Over Raised Shoulder

This is self-mimicry of the rounded female breasts. Figure 116 also makes use of dilated pupils, the head toss, exposed wrists, sideways glance, artificially extended gaze, wet lips, head up and fondling a cylindrical object, all of which are intended to generate desire for a particular brand of cigarette.

Female Leg-Cross Gestures

Men often sit with their legs apart in an aggressive crotch display, whereas women use leg crossing as protection for their delicate genital area. Women use three basic positions to communicate a courting attitude.

With the knee point (Figure 118), one leg is tucked under the other and points to the person whom she finds interesting. This is a very relaxed position which takes the formality out of a conversation and gives the opportunity for a fleeting exposure of the thighs.

Figure 118   *The knee point*

The shoe fondle (Figure 119) also indicates a relaxed attitude and has the phallic effect of thrusting the foot in and out of the shoe, which can drive some men wild.

Figure 119 *The shoe gives a clue*

Most men agree that the leg twine (Figure 120) is the most appealing sitting position a woman can take. It is a gesture that women consciously use to attract attention. Dr. Scheflen states that one leg is pressed firmly against the other to give the appearance of high muscle tone which, as previously mentioned, is a condition that the body takes when a person is ready for sexual performance.

Figure 120   *The leg twine*

Other signals used by women include crossing and un-
crossing the legs slowly in front of the man and gently stroking the thighs with her hand, indicating a desire to be
touched. This is often accompanied by speaking in a low
voice.

Figure 121 *Without referring to what you have just read, how many courting signals and gestures can you see?*

Eleven

Cigars, Cigarettes, Pipes and Glasses

Smoking Gestures

Smoking is an outward manifestation of an inner turmoil or conflict and has little to do with nicotine addiction. It is one of the displacement activities that people in today's high-pressure society use to release the tensions that build up from social and business encounters. For example, most people experience inner tension while waiting outside the dentist's office to have a tooth removed. While a smoker will cover up his anxiety by smoking, non-smokers perform other rituals such as grooming, nail biting, finger and foot tapping, cuff-link adjusting, head scratching, taking a ring off and putting it back on, playing with a tie and demonstrating numerous other gestures that tell us the person needs reassurance.

Smoking gestures can play an important part in assessing a person's attitude, as they are usually performed in a predict-able, ritualistic manner that can give us important clues to the person's attitude.

Pipe Smokers

Pipe smokers perform a cleaning, lighting, tapping, filling, packing and puffing ritual with their pipes and this is a very useful way to help relieve tension when they are under pressure. Sales research has shown that pipe smokers usually take longer to make a decision to buy than do cigarette smokers or non-smokers and that the pipe ritual is performed most often during the tense moments of the sales presentation. Pipe smokers, it seems, are people who like to stall decision-making and who can do so in an unobtrusive and socially acceptable way. If you want a quick decision from a pipe smoker, hide his pipe before the interview.

Cigarette Smokers

Like pipe smoking, cigarette smoking is a displacement of inner tension and allows time to stall, but the cigarette smoker generally reaches his decision faster than the pipe smoker. The pipe smoker is, in effect, a cigarette smoker who needs more time to stall in making decisions than his cigarettes allow. The cigarette ritual involves tapping, twisting, flicking, waving and other mini-gestures indicating that the person is experiencing more tension than may be normal.

One particular signal indicates whether the person has a positive or negative attitude towards his circumstances; the direction in which the smoke is exhaled, whether it is up or down. A person who is feeling positive, superior or confident will blow the smoke in an upward direction most of the time. Conversely, a person in a negative, secretive or suspicious frame of mind will blow the smoke down most of the time. Blowing down and from the corner of the mouth indicates an even more negative or secretive attitude. This, of course, assumes that the smoker is not blowing the smoke upwards to avoid offending others; in that case, he could have blown the smoke in either direction.

In motion pictures, the leader of a motorcycle gang or criminal syndicate is usually portrayed as a tough, aggressive person who, as he smokes, tilts his head back sharply and with controlled precision blows the smoke towards the ceiling to

Figure 122   *Smoke up: confident, superior, positive*

Figure 123   *Smoke down: negative, secretive, suspicious*

demonstrate his superiority to the rest of the gang. In contrast, Humphrey Bogart was often cast as a gangster or criminal who always held his cigarette inverted in his hand and blew the smoke down from the corner of his mouth as he planned a jail break or other devious activity. There also appears to be a relationship between how positive or negative the person feels and the speed at which he or she exhales the smoke. The faster the smoke is blown upwards the more superior or confident the person feels; the faster it is blown down, the more negative he feels.

If a card player who is smoking is dealt a good hand, he is likely to blow the smoke upwards, whereas a poor hand may cause him to blow it downwards. Some card players use a 'poker face' when playing cards as a method of not displaying any body signals that may give them away, while other players like to be actors and use misleading body language to lull the other players into a false sense of security. If, for example, a poker player were dealt four aces and he wanted to bluff the other players, he could throw the cards face down on the table in disgust and then curse, swear or fold his arms and put on a non-verbal display that would indicate that he had been dealt a poor hand. But then he quietly sits back and draws on his cigarette and blows the smoke upwards! Having read this chapter, you will now be aware that it would be unwise for the other players to play the next hand as they would probably be beaten. Observation of smoking gestures in selling shows that when a smoker is asked to buy, those who have reached a positive decision blow the smoke upwards, whereas those who have decided not to buy blow it downwards. The alert salesperson, seeing the smoke being blown downwards during the close of a sale could quickly resell the customer on all the benefits he would receive by purchasing the product, to allow the customer time to reconsider his decision.

Blowing smoke out through the nostrils is a sign of a superior, confident individual. The smoke is blown downwards only because of the physical location of the nostrils and the person often tilts his head back in a 'looking down his nose' position. If the person's head is down as he nose-blows the smoke, he is angry and is trying to look ferocious, like an angry bull.

Cigar Smokers

Cigars have always been used as a means of displaying superiority because of their cost and size. The big-time business executive, the gang leader and people in high-status positions often smoke cigars. Cigars are used to celebrate a victory or achievement such as the birth of a baby, a wedding, clinching a business deal or winning the lottery. It is not surprising that most of the smoke exhaled by cigar smokers is upwards. I recently attended a celebration dinner where cigars were distributed freely and it was interesting to note that of 400 recorded cigar smoke exhalations, 320 were in an upward direction.

General Smoking Signals

The continual tapping of a cigar or cigarette end on the ashtray shows that an inner conflict is taking place and that you may need to reassure the smoker. Here, too, is an interesting smoking phenomenon. Most smokers smoke their cigarette down to a certain length before extinguishing it in the ashtray. If the smoker lights a cigarette and suddenly extinguishes it earlier than he normally would, he has signaled his decision to terminate the conversation. Watching for this termination signal can allow you to take control or to close the conversation, making it appear that it was your idea to end it.

Gestures with Glasses

Almost every artificial aid used by man gives its user an opportunity to perform many revealing gestures and this is certainly the case with those who wear glasses. One of the most common gestures is placing one arm of the frame in the mouth (Figure 124).

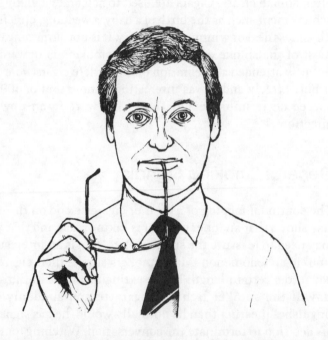

Figure 124   *Stalling for time*

Desmond Morris says that the act of putting objects against the lips or in the mouth is a momentary attempt by the person to relive the security he experienced as a baby at his mother's breast, which means that glasses-in-mouth is essentially a reassurance gesture. Smokers use their cigarettes for the same reason, and the child sucks his thumb.

Stalling

Like pipe smoking, the glasses-in-mouth gesture can be used to stall or delay a decision. In negotiating, it has been found that this gesture appears most frequently at the close of the discussion when the person has been asked for a decision. The act of continually taking the glasses off and cleaning the lenses is another method used by people who wear glasses to gain time for a decision. When this gesture is seen immediately after a decision has been asked for, silence is the best tactic.

The gestures that follow this stall gesture signal the person's intention and allow an alert negotiator to respond accordingly. For example, if the person puts the glasses back on, this often means that he wants to 'see' the facts again, whereas folding the glasses and putting them away signals an intention to terminate the conversation.

Peering Over Glasses

Actors in the motion pictures made during the 1920s and 1930s used this peering gesture to portray a critical or judgmental person such as the master of an English public school. Often the person may be wearing reading glasses and finds it more convenient to look over the tops, rather than removing them to look at the other person. Whoever is on the receiving end of this look may feel as though he is being judged or scrutinized. Looking over the glasses can be a very costly mistake, as the listener inevitably responds to this look with folded arms, crossed legs and a correspondingly negative attitude. People with glasses should remove them when speaking and put them back on to listen. This not only relaxes the other person but allows the wearer to have control of the conversation. The listener quickly learns that when the glasses are off he must not interrupt the speaker, and when they are put back on he had better start talking.

Figure 125 *The aggressor*

Twelve

Territorial and Ownership Gestures

Territorial Gestures

People lean against other people or objects to show a territorial claim to that object or person. Leaning can also be used as a method of dominance or intimidation when the object being leaned on belongs to someone else. For example, if you are going to take a photograph of a friend and his new car, boat, home or other personal belonging, you will inevitably find that he leans against his newly acquired property, putting his foot on it or his arm around it (Figure 127). When he touches the property, it becomes an extension of his body and in this way he shows others that it belongs to him. Young lovers continually hold hands or put their arms around one another in public and social situations to show others the claim that they have on each other. The business executive puts his feet on his desk or desk drawers or leans against his office doorway to show his claim to that office and its furnishings.

However, an easy way to intimidate someone is to lean against, sit upon or use their possessions without their permission. In addition to the obvious abuses of another's territory or possessions such as sitting at his desk or borrowing his car without asking, there are other very subtle intimidation techniques. One is to lean against the doorway in another's office or to inadvertently sit in his chair.

Figure 126   *Staking a claim*

Figure 127   *Gesture showing pride of ownership*

As already mentioned, a salesperson calling on a customer at his home is well advised to ask him 'Which seat is yours?' before he sits down, as sitting in the wrong chair intimidates the customer and puts him off, which can have a detrimental effect on the chance of a successful sale.

Some people, like the man shown in Figure 128, are habitual doorway leaners and go through life intimidating most people from the first introduction. These people are well advised to practice an erect stance with palms visible to make a favorable impression on others. People form 90 percent of their opinion about you in the first ninety seconds of meeting you, and you never get a second chance to make a first impression!

Figure 128   *The intimidator*

Ownership Gestures

Management personnel are particularly guilty of continually using the following gestures. It has been noted that employees who have been newly appointed to management positions suddenly begin to use them, despite the fact that they seldom used them prior to their promotion.

It would be normal to assume that the position of the man in Figure 129 reflects an easy-going, relaxed and carefree attitude, because that is in fact what it is. The leg-over-chair gesture not only signifies the man's ownership of that particular chair or space, but also signals that customary etiquettes may be relaxed.

It is common to see two close friends seated like this, laughing and joking with each other, but let's consider the impact and meaning of this gesture in different circumstances. Take this typical situation: an employee has a personal problem and he goes into the boss's office to ask his advice on a possible solution. As the employee explains, he leans forward in the chair, his hands on his knees, his face down and looking dejected and his tone of voice lowered. The boss listens intently, sitting motionless, then suddenly leans back in his chair and puts one leg over the arm. In these circumstances the boss's attitude has changed to lack of concern or indifference because of his carefree gesture. In other words, he has little concern for the employee or his problem and he may even feel that his time is being wasted with the 'same old story'.

A further question needs to be answered: what is the boss indifferent about? He may have considered the employee's problem, decided that it's not really a major one and he may even have become uninterested in or indifferent towards the employee. While he remains in the leg-over-chair position, he will probably have a concerned look on his face throughout the discussion to cover up his lack of interest. He may even terminate the discussion by telling his employee that he need not worry and that the problem will simply go away. When the employee leaves the office, the boss may breathe a sigh of relief and say to himself, 'Thank heavens he's gone!' and take his leg off the chair.

If the boss's chair has no arms (which is unlikely; this is usually the visitor's chair) he may be seen with one or both feet on the desk (Figure 130). If his superior enters the office, it is unlikely that the boss would use such an obvious territorial/ownership gesture, but would resort to more subtle versions such as putting his foot on the bottom drawer of his desk, or, if there are no drawers in the desk, placing his foot hard against the leg of the desk to stake his claim to it.

Figure 129 *Lack of concern*

These gestures can be quite annoying if they occur during negotiation, and it is vital that the person should change to a different position because the longer he stays in the leg-over-chair or feet-on-desk position, the longer he will have an indifferent or hostile attitude. An easy way to do this is to hand him something that he cannot reach and ask him to lean across and look at it, or, if you and he have a similar sense of humor, tell him he has a split in his trousers.

Figure 130   *Claiming ownership of the desk*

Thirteen

Mirroring

The next time you attend a social function or go to a place where people meet and interact, take note of the number of people who have adopted the identical gestures and posture of the person with whom they are talking. This 'mirroring' is a means by which one person tells the other that he is in agreement with his ideas and attitudes. By this method, one is non-verbally saying to the other, 'As you can see, I think the same as you, so I will copy your posture and gestures.'

This unconscious mimicry is quite interesting to observe. Take for example, the two men standing at the hotel bar in Figure 131. They have mirrored each other's gestures and it is reasonable to assume that they are discussing a topic upon which they have the same thoughts and feelings. If one man uncrosses his arms and legs or stands on the other foot, the other will follow. If one puts his hand in his pocket, the other will copy and this mimicry will continue for as long as the two men are in agreement. This copying also occurs among good friends or people at the same status level and it is common to see married couples walk, stand, sit and move in identical ways. Scheflen found that people who are strangers studiously avoid holding mutual positions. The significance of mirroring can be one of the most important non-verbal lessons we can learn, for this is one way that others tell us that they agree with us or like us. It is also a way for us to tell others that we like them, by simply copying their gestures.

Figure 131 *Thinking alike*

If an employer wishes to develop an immediate rapport and create a relaxed atmosphere with an employee, he need only copy the employee's posture to achieve this end. Similarly, an up-and-coming employee may be seen copying his boss's gestures in an attempt to show agreement. Using this knowledge, it is possible to influence a face-to-face encounter by copying the positive gestures and postures of the other person. This has the effect of putting the other person in a receptive and relaxed frame of mind, as he can 'see' that you understand his point of view (Figure 132).

Figure 132 *Copying the other person's gestures to gain acceptance*

When I was selling insurance I found this a very effective technique for a 'cold' prospective customer. I deliberately copied each movement the prospective customer made until I felt I had established a strong enough rapport to allow the presentation to proceed. Invariably, if the prospect began copying my gestures, a sale would result.

However, before copying the other person's gestures when negotiating, it is vital that your relationship with that person be taken into consideration. Let's say, for example, that the junior clerk of a large corporation has asked for a pay raise and is called into the manager's office. As he walks in, the manager asks him to sit down and then assumes a superiority T-cross gesture (Figure 93) and a figure 4 leg lock (Figure 78) while he leans back in his chair to show the clerk his superior, dominant and competitive attitude. What would happen if the clerk then copied the manager's dominant posture while discussing his potential salary raise (Figure 133)?

Even if the clerk's verbal communication were on the subordinate level, the manager would feel intimidated and even insulted by the clerk's non-verbal behavior and the clerk's job could be in jeopardy. This maneuver is a highly effective method of disarming 'superior' types who try to take the control. Accountants, lawyers and management personnel are known for assuming these postures in the presence of people whom they consider inferior. By taking the same posture, you can effectively disconcert them and force them to change their position, allowing you to take the control.

Figure 133 *The non-verbal challenge*

Research shows that when the leader of a group uses certain gestures and positions, subordinates copy them. Leaders also tend to be the first of a group to walk through a doorway and they like to sit on the end of a couch or bench seat rather than in the center. When a group of executives walk into a room, the boss usually goes first. When executives are seated in the board room, the boss usually sits at the head of the table, often farthest from the door. If the boss sits with a hands-behind-head T-cross gesture (Figure 93), his subordinates will copy.

People who sell to married couples in their homes are well advised to watch the couple's gestures, to see who initiates the gestures and who follows.

For example, if the husband is doing all the talking and the wife sits there saying nothing, but you notice that the husband copies his wife's gestures, you will inevitably find that she makes the decisions and writes the check, so it is a good idea to direct your presentation to her.

Fourteen

Body Lowering and Status

Historically, lowering the height of one's body in front of another person has been used as a means of establishing superior/subordinate relationships. We refer to a member of Royalty as 'Your Highness', whereas individuals who commit unsavory acts are called 'low'. The protest rally speaker stands on a soapbox to be higher than everyone else, the judge sits higher than the rest of the court, those who live in a penthouse command more authority than those who live at ground level and some cultures divide their social classes into the 'upper class' and 'lower class'.

Despite what many people would like to believe, tall people command more authority than short people, but height can also be detrimental to some aspects of one-to-one communication where you need to 'talk on the same level' or have an 'eye-to-eye' discussion with another person.

Most women curtsy when they meet Royalty and men incline their heads or remove their hats, making themselves appear smaller than the Royal person. The modern salute is a relic of the act of body lowering. The more humble or subordinate an individual feels towards another, the lower he stoops his body. In business, the people who continually 'bow' to the management are labeled with such derogatory name tags as 'bootlickers' or 'crawlers'.

Unfortunately, little can be done to help people become

taller or shorter, so let us explore some useful applications of height.

It is possible to avoid intimidating others by consciously making yourself appear smaller in relation to them, so let us examine the non-verbal aspects of the situation in which you have been speeding in your car and are stopped by the police. In these circumstances, the officer may regard you as an adversary as he approaches your vehicle, and a driver's usual reaction is to remain in the car, wind the window down and make excuses for having exceeded the speed limit. The non-verbal negatives of this behavior are: (1) The officer is forced to leave his territory (the patrol car) and come across to your territory (your vehicle). (2) Assuming that you have in fact broken the speed limit, your excuses may represent an attack to the officer. (3) By remaining in your car, you create a barrier between yourself and the policeman.

Considering that under these circumstances the police officer is obviously in a superior position to you, this type of behavior only serves to make things go from bad to worse and your chances of being booked are increased. Instead, try this if you are flagged down: (1) Get immediately out of your car (your territory) and go over to the police officer's car (his territory). In this way he is not inconvenienced by having to leave his territory. (2) Stoop your body over so that you are smaller than he is. (3) Lower your own status by telling the officer how foolish and irresponsible you are and raise his status by thanking him for pointing out the error of your ways and telling him that you realize how difficult his job must be with fools like you around. (4) With your palms out, in a trembling voice, ask him not to give you a ticket. This type of behavior shows the police officer that you are not a threat to him and often causes him to take the role of an angry parent, in which case he gives you a stern warning and tells you to be on your way—without a speeding ticket! When this technique is used as directed, it can save you from being booked more than 50 percent of the time.

The same technique can be used to calm an irate customer

who is returning some faulty goods to a retail store. In this case, the counter represents a barrier between the store owner and the customer. Control of an irate customer would be difficult if the storekeeper remained on his own side of the counter, and this staking-out of territory would make the customer angrier. The best approach would be for the storekeeper to come around to the customer's side of the counter with his body stooped over and palms visible and to use the same technique as was used with the police officer.

Figure 134 *'Please don't book me . . .'*

Interestingly, there are some circumstances under which lowering the body can be a dominance signal. This is where you slouch down and make yourself comfortable in an easy chair in another person's home while the owner is standing. It is the complete informality on the other person's territory that communicates the dominant or aggressive attitude.

It is also important to remember that a person will always be superior on his own territory, especially in his own home, and submissive gestures and behavior are very effective methods for getting the person to side with you.

Fifteen

Pointers

Have you ever had the feeling that someone to whom you are talking would rather be somewhere else than with you, even though he or she seems to be enjoying your company? A still photograph of that scene would probably reveal the following: (1) The person's head is turned towards you and facial signals such as smiling and nodding are evident. (2) The person's body and feet are pointing *away* from you, either towards another person or towards an exit. The direction in which a person points his or her torso or feet is a signal of where he or she would prefer to be going.

Figure 135 shows two men talking in a doorway. The man on the left is trying to hold the other man's attention, but his listener wishes to continue in the direction to which his body is pointing, although his head is turned to acknowledge the other man's presence. It is only when the man on the right turns his body towards the other that a mutually interesting conversation can take place.

It is noticeable that often in negotiations, when one person has decided to terminate the negotiation or wants to leave, he will turn his body or swing his feet to point towards the nearest exit. If you see these signals during a face-to-face encounter, you should do something to get the person involved and interested or else terminate the conversation on your terms, which allows you to maintain the control.

Figure 135   *The body shows where the mind wants to go*

Angles and Triangles

Open Formation

In an earlier chapter, we stated that the physical distance between people is related to their degree of intimacy. The angle at which people orient their bodies also gives many non-verbal clues to their attitudes and relationships. For example, people in most English-speaking countries stand with their bodies oriented to form an angle of 90 degrees during ordinary social intercourse. Figure 136 shows two men with their bodies angled towards an imaginary third point to form a triangle. This also serves as a non-verbal invitation for a third person to join in the conversation by standing at the third point. The two men in Figure 136 are displaying similar status by holding similar gestures and posture and the angle formed by their torsos indicates that an impersonal conversation is probably taking place. The formation of the triangle invites a third person of similar status to join the conversation. When a fourth person is accepted into the group a square will be formed and for a fifth person, either a circle or two triangles.

Figure 136   *Open triangular position*

Closed Formation

When intimacy or privacy is required by two people, the angle formed by their torsos decreases from 90 degrees down to 0 degrees. A man wishing to attract a female partner uses this ploy, as well as other courtship gestures, when he makes his play for her. Not only does he point his body towards her, but he also closes the distance between them as he moves into her intimate zone. To accept his approach, she need only orient her torso angle to 0 degrees and allow him to enter her territory. The distance between two people standing in the closed formation is usually less than that of the open formation.

Figure 137   *Direct body pointing in the closed formation*

In addition to the usual courtship displays, both parties may mirror each other's gestures if they are interested in each other. Like some other courtship gestures, the closed formation can be used as a non-verbal challenge between people who are hostile to each other (see Figure 103).

Inclusion and Exclusion Techniques

Both the open triangular position and the closed position are used to include or exclude another person from the con-

versation. Figure 138 shows the triangular formation taken
by the first two to show acceptance of the third.

Figure 138 *Open triangular position signaling acceptance*

When a third person wishes to join two others who are
standing in a closed formation, he may be invited to join the
conversation only when the other two orient their torsos
towards a mutual third point to form the triangle. If the third
person is not accepted, the others will hold the closed formation position and turn only their heads towards him or her as
a sign of recognition of the third person's presence, but the
direction of their torsos shows that he is not invited to remain (Figure 139).

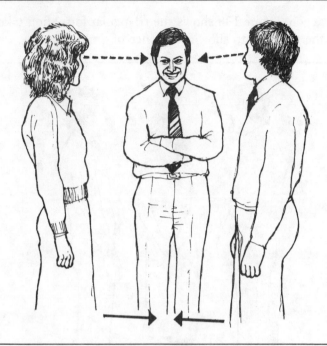

Figure 139   *Third person not accepted by first two*

Often a conversation among three people may begin in the open triangular formation but eventually two may take the closed formation position to exclude the third person (Figure 139). This group formation is a clear signal to the third person that he should leave the group to avoid embarrassment.

Seated Body Pointing

Crossing the knees towards another person is a sign of acceptance or interest in that person. If the other person also becomes interested, he or she will cross knees towards the first person, as shown in Figure 140. As the two people become more involved with each other they will begin to copy each other's movements and gestures, as is the case in Figure 140, and a closed formation results that excludes all others, such as the man on the right. The only way in which the man on the right could participate in the conversation would be to move a chair to a position in front of the couple and attempt to form a triangle, or take some other action to break the formation.

Figure 140 *Body pointing is used to exclude the man on the right*

Interviewing Two People

Let us assume that you, person C, are going to interview or talk to persons A and B, and let us say that by either choice or circumstance you are sitting in a triangular position at a round table. Let us also assume that person A is very talkative and asks many questions and that person B remains silent throughout. When A asks you a question, how can you answer him and carry on a conversation without making B feel excluded? Use this simple but highly effective inclusion technique: when A asks a question, look at him as you begin to answer, then turn your head towards B, then back to A, then to B again until you make your final statement, looking at A (who asked the question) again as you finish your sentence. This technique lets B feel involved in the conversation and is particularly useful if you need to have B on your side.

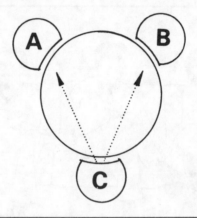

Figure 141   *Two-person interview*

Foot Pointing

Not only do the feet serve as pointers, indicating the direction in which a person would like to go, but they are also used to point at people who are interesting or attractive. Imagine that you are at a social function and you notice a group of three men and one very attractive woman (Figure 142). The conversation seems to be dominated by the men and the woman is just listening. Then you notice something interesting—the men all have one foot pointing towards the woman. With this simple non-verbal cue, the men are all telling the woman that they are interested in her. Subconsciously, the woman sees the foot gestures and is likely to remain with the group for as long as she is receiving this attention. In Figure

142 she is standing with both feet together in the neutral position and she may eventually point one foot toward the man whom she finds the most attractive or interesting. You will also notice that she is giving a sideways glance to the man who is using the thumbs-in-belt gesture.

Figure 142 *Feet signaling what's on the owner's mind*

Seated-Body Formations

Take the following situation: you are in a supervisory capacity and are about to counsel a subordinate whose work performance has been unsatisfactory and erratic. To achieve this objective, you feel that you will need to use direct questions that require direct answers and may put the subordinate under pressure. At times you will also need to show the subordinate that you understand his feelings and, from time to time, that you agree with his thoughts or actions. How can you non-verbally convey these attitudes using body formations? Leaving aside interview and questioning techniques for these illustrations, consider the following points: (1) The fact that the counseling session is in your office and that you are the boss allows you to move from behind your desk to the employee's side of the desk (the cooperative position) and still maintain unspoken control. (2) The subordinate should be seated on a chair with fixed legs and no arms, one that forces

Figure 143   *Open triangular formation*

him to use body gestures and postures that will give you a better understanding of his attitudes. (3) You should be sitting on a swivel chair with arms, giving you more control and letting you eliminate some of your own giveaway gestures by allowing you to move around.

There are three main angle formations that can be used.

Like the standing triangular position, the open triangular formation lends an informal, relaxed attitude to the meeting and is a good position in which to open a counseling session (Figure 143). You can show non-verbal agreement with the subordinate from this position by copying his movements and gestures. As they do in the standing position, both torsos

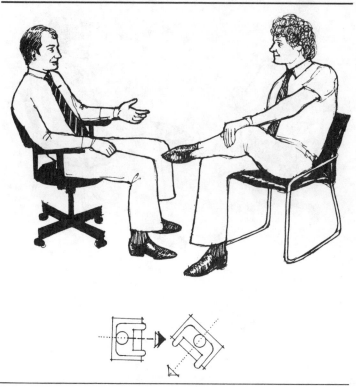

Figure 144 *Direct body point*

point to a third mutual point to form a triangle; this can show mutual agreement.

By turning your chair to point your body directly at your subordinate (Figure 144) you are non-verbally telling him that you want direct answers to your questions. Combine this position with the business gaze (Figure 106) and reduced body and facial gestures and your subject will feel tremendous non-verbal pressure. If, for example, after you have asked him a question, he rubs his eye and mouth and looks away when

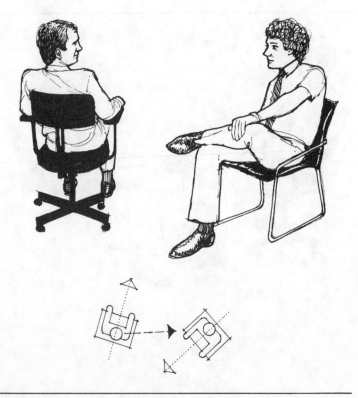

Figure 145 *The right angle position*

he answers, swing your chair to point directly at him and say, 'Are you sure about that?' This simple movement exerts non-verbal pressure on him and can force him to tell the truth.

When you position your body at a right angle away from your subject, you take the pressure off the interview (Figure 145). This is an excellent position from which to ask delicate or embarrassing questions, encouraging more open answers to your questions without any pressure coming from you. If the nut you are trying to crack is a difficult one, you may need to revert to the direct body point technique to get to the facts.

Summary

If you want a person to have rapport with you, use the triangular position and, when you need to exert non-verbal pressure, use the direct body point. The right angle position allows the other person to think and act independently, without non-verbal pressure from you. Few people have ever considered the effect of body pointing in influencing the attitudes and the responses of others.

These techniques take much practice to master but they can become 'natural' movements before long. If you deal with others for a living, mastery of body point and swivel chair techniques are very useful skills to acquire. In your day-to-day encounters with others, foot pointing, body pointing and positive gesture clusters such as open arms, visible palms, leaning forward, head tilting and smiling can make it easy for others not only to enjoy your company, but to be influenced by your point of view.

Sixteen

Desks, Tables and Seating Arrangements

Table-Seating Positions

Strategic positioning in relation to other people is an effective way to obtain cooperation from them. Aspects of their attitude toward you can be revealed in the position they take in relation to you.

Mark Knapp, in his book *Non-Verbal Communication in Human Interaction*, noted that, although there is a general formula for interpretation of seating positions, the environment may have an effect on the position chosen. Research conducted with white, middle-class Americans showed that seating positions in the public bar of a hotel can vary from the seating positions taken in a high-class restaurant and that the direction in which the seats are facing and the distance between tables can have a distorting influence on seating behavior. For example, intimate couples prefer to sit side-by-side wherever possible, but in a crowded restaurant where the tables are close together this is not possible and the couples are forced to sit opposite each other in what is normally a defensive position.

Because of a wide range of moderating circumstances, the following examples relate primarily to seating arrangements in an office environment with a standard rectangular desk.

Person B can take four basic seating positions in relation to person A.

B1: The corner position
B2: The cooperative position
B3: The competitive/defensive position
B4: The independent position

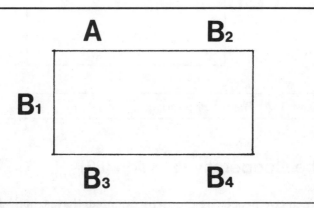

Figure 146   *Basic seating positions*

The Corner Position (B1)

This position is normally used by people who are engaged in friendly,. casual conversation. The position allows for unlimited eye contact and the opportunity to use numerous gestures and to observe the gestures of the other person. The corner of the desk provides a partial barrier should one person begin to feel threatened, and this position avoids a territorial division on the top of the table. The most successful strategic position from which a salesperson can deliver a presentation to a new customer is by position B1 assuming A is the buyer. By simply moving the chair to position B1 you can relieve a tense atmosphere and increase the chances of a favorable negotiation.

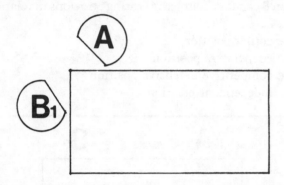

Figure 147   *The corner position*

The Cooperative Position (B2)

When two people are mutually oriented, that is, both thinking alike or working on a task together, this position usually occurs. It is one of the most strategic positions for presenting a case and having it accepted. The trick is, however, for B to be able to take this position without A feeling as though his territory has been invaded. This is also a highly successful position to take when a third party is introduced into the negotiation by B, the salesperson. Say, for example, that a salesperson was having a second interview with a client and the salesperson introduced a technical expert. The following strategy would be the most suitable.

The technical expert is seated at position C opposite customer A. The salesperson can sit either at position B2 (cooperative) or B1 (corner). This allows the salesperson to be 'on the client's side' and to question the technician on behalf of the client. This position is often known as 'siding with the opposition'.

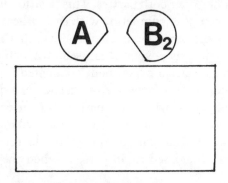

Figure 148   *The cooperative position*

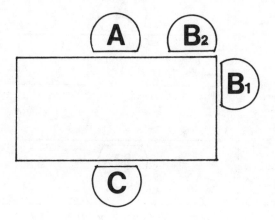

Figure 149   *Introducing a third person*

The Competitive/Defensive Position (B3)

Sitting across the table from a person can create a defensive, competitive atmosphere and can lead to each party taking a firm stand on his point of view because the table becomes a solid barrier between both parties. This position is taken by people who are either competing with each other or if one is reprimanding the other. It can also establish that a superior/subordinate role exists when it is used in A's office.

Argyle noted that an experiment conducted in a doctor's office showed that the presence or absence of a desk had a significant effect on whether a patient was at ease or not. Only 10 percent of the patients were perceived to be at ease when the doctor's desk was present and the doctor sat behind it. This figure increased to 55 percent when the desk was absent.

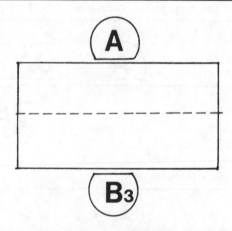

Figure 150   *Competitive/defensive position*

If B is seeking to persuade A, the competitive/defensive position reduces the chance of a successful negotiation unless B is deliberately sitting opposite as part of a pre-planned strategy. For example, it may be that A is a manager who must severely reprimand employee B, and the competitive position can strengthen the reprimand. On the other hand, it may be necessary for B to make A feel superior and so B deliberately sits directly opposite A.

Whatever line of business you are in, if it involves dealing with people, you are in the influencing business and your objective should always be to see the other person's point of view, to put him or her at ease and make him or her feel right about dealing with you; the competitive position does not lead towards this end. More cooperation will be gained from the corner and cooperative positions than will ever be achieved from the competitive position. Conversations are shorter and more specific in this position than from any other.

Whenever people sit directly opposite each other across a table, they unconsciously divide it into two equal territories. Each claims half as his own territory and will reject the other's encroaching upon it. Two people seated competitively at a restaurant table will mark their territorial boundaries with the salt, pepper, sugar bowl and napkins.

Here is a simple test that you can conduct at a restaurant which demonstrates how a person will react to invasion of his territory. I recently took a salesman to lunch to offer him a contract with our company. We sat at a small rectangular restaurant table which was too small to allow me to take the corner position so I was forced to sit in the competitive position.

The usual dining items were on the table: ashtray, salt and pepper shakers, napkins and a menu. I picked up the menu, read it, and then pushed it across into the other man's territory. He picked it up, read it, and then placed it back in the center of the table to his right. I then picked it up again, read it, and placed it back in his territory. He had been leaning forward at this point and this subtle invasion made him sit back. The ashtray was in the middle of the table and, as I ashed my cigarette, I pushed it into his territory. He then ashed his own cigarette and pushed the ashtray back to the center of the table once again. Again, quite casually, I ashed my cigarette and pushed the ashtray back to his side. I then slowly pushed the sugar bowl from the middle to his side and he began to show discomfort. Then I pushed the salt and pepper shakers across the center line. By this time, he was squirming around in his seat as though he was sitting on an ant's nest and a light film of sweat began to form on his brow. When I pushed the napkins across to his side it was all too much and he excused himself and went to the toilet. On his return, I also excused myself. When I returned to the table I found that all the table items had been pushed back to the center line!

This simple, effective game demonstrates the tremendous resistance that a person has to the invasion of his territory. It should now be obvious why the competitive seating arrangement should be avoided in any negotiation or discussion.

There will be occasions on which it may be difficult or inappropriate to take the corner position to present your case. Let us assume that you have a visual presentation; a book, quotation or sample to present to another person who is sitting behind a rectangular desk. First, place the article on the table (Figure 151). The other person will lean forward and look at it, take it into his territory or push it back into your territory.

Figure 151   *Paper placed on territorial line*

Figure 152 *Taking paper into his territory signals non-verbal acceptance*

Figure 153 *Non-verbal agreement to enter buyer's territory*

If he leans forward to look at it, you must deliver your presentation from where you sit as this action non-verbally tells you that he does not want you on his side of the desk. If he takes it into his territory this gives you the opportunity to ask permission to enter his territory and take either the corner or cooperative positions (Figure 153). If, however, he pushes it back, you're in trouble! The golden rule is never to encroach on the other person's territory unless you have been given verbal or non-verbal permission to do so or you will put them off.

The Independent Position (B4)

This is the position taken by people when they do not wish to interact with each other; it occurs in such places as a library, park bench or restaurant. It signifies lack of interest and can even be interpreted as hostile by the other person if the territorial boundaries are invaded. This position should be avoided where open discussion between A and B is required.

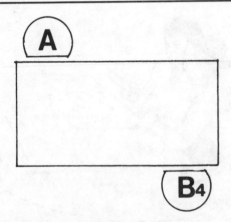

Figure 154 *Independent position*

Square, Round, Rectangular Tables

Square Table (Formal)

As previously mentioned, square tables create a competitive or defensive relationship between people of equal status. Square tables are ideal for having short, to-the-point conversations or to create a superior/subordinate relationship. The most cooperation usually comes from the person seated beside you and the one on the right tends to be more cooperative than the one on the left. The most resistance usually comes from the person seated directly opposite.

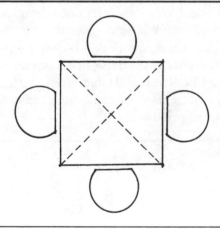

Figure 155   *Square table (formal)*

Round Table (Informal)

King Arthur used the Round Table as an attempt to give each of his knights an equal amount of authority and status. A round table creates an atmosphere of relaxed informality and is ideal for promoting discussion among people who are of equal status as each person can claim the same amount of table territory. Removing the table and sitting in a circle also promotes the same result. Unfortunately, King Arthur was unaware that if the status of one person is higher than the others in the group it alters the power and authority of each other individual. The king held the most power at the Round Table and this meant that the knights seated on either side of him were non-verbally granted the next highest amount of power, the one on his right having a little more power than the one on the left, and the amount of power diminished relative to the distance that each knight was seated away from the king.

Consequently, the knight seated directly across the table from King Arthur was, in effect, in the competitive/defensive position and was likely to be the one who gave the most trouble. Many of today's business executives use both square and round tables. The square desk, which is usually the work desk, is used for business activity, brief conversations, reprimands and the like. The round table, often a coffee table with wrap-around seating, is used to create an informal relaxed atmosphere or to persuade.

Figure 156 *Round table (informal)*

Rectangular Tables

On a rectangular table, position A has always commanded the most influence. In a meeting of people of equal status the person sitting at position A will have the most influence, assuming that he does not have his back to the door. If A's back were facing the door, the person seated at B would be the most influential and would be strong competition for A. Assuming that A was in the best power position, person B has the next most authority, then C, then D. This information makes it possible to structure power plays at meetings by placing name badges on the seats where you want each person to sit so that you may have the maximum influence over them.

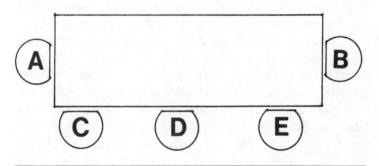

Figure 157 *Positioning at a rectangular table*

The Dining Table at Home

The choice of the shape of a family dining room table can give a clue to the power distribution in that family, assuming that the dining room could have accommodated a table of any shape and that the table shape was selected after considerable thought. 'Open' families go for round tables, 'closed' families select square tables and 'authoritative' types select rectangular tables.

Getting a Decision over Dinner

Bearing in mind what has already been said about human territories and the use of square, rectangular and round tables, let us now look at the dynamics of taking a person to dinner where the objective is to obtain a favorable response to a proposition. Let us examine the factors that can build a positive atmosphere, discuss their origin and potential and examine the background of man's feeding behavior.

Anthropologists tell us that man's origin was that of a tree-dweller who was strictly vegetarian, his diet consisting of roots, leaves, berries, fruit and the like. About a million years ago, he came out of the trees onto the plains to become a hunter of prey. Prior to his becoming a land dweller, man's eating habits were those of the monkeys—involving continual nibbling throughout the day. Each individual was entirely responsible for his own survival and for obtaining his own food. As a hunter, however, he needed the cooperation of other individuals to capture large prey, so large cooperative hunting groups were formed. Each group would leave at sunrise to hunt throughout the day and return at dusk with the day's spoils. These were then divided equally among the hunters, who would eat inside a communal cave.

At the entrance to the cave a fire was lit to ward off dangerous animals and to provide warmth. Each caveman sat with his back against the wall of the cave to avoid the possibility of being attacked from behind while he was engrossed in eating his meal. The only sounds that were heard were the gnashing and gnawing of teeth and the crackle of the fire. This ancient process of food sharing at dusk around an open fire was the beginning of a social event that modern man re-enacts in the form of barbecues, cookouts and dinner parties.

Modern man also reacts and behaves at these events in much the same way as he did over a million years ago.

Now to our restaurant or dinner party. A positive decision in your favor is easier to obtain when your prospect is relaxed, free of tension and his or her defensive barriers have been lowered. To achieve this end, and keeping in mind what has already been said about our ancestors, a few simple rules need to be followed.

First, whether you are dining at your home or at a restaurant, have your prospect seated with his back to a solid wall or screen. Research shows that respiration, heart rate, brain wave frequencies and blood pressure rapidly increase when a person sits with his back to an open space, particularly where others are moving about. Tension is further increased if the person's back is towards an open door or a window at ground level. Next, the lights should be dimmed and muffled background music played. Many top restaurants have an open fireplace or facsimile near the entrance of the restaurant to recreate the fire that burned at the ancient cave feasts. It would be best to use a round table and to have your prospect's view of other people obscured by a screen or large green plant if you are to have a captive audience.

It is far easier to obtain a favorable decision under these circumstances than it will ever be in restaurants that have bright lighting, tables and chairs placed in open areas and the banging of plates, knives and forks. Top restaurants use these types of relaxation techniques to extract large amounts of money from their customer's wallets for ordinary food, and men have been using them for thousands of years to create a romantic atmosphere for the benefit of women.

Seventeen

Power Plays

Power Plays with Chairs

Have you ever been for a job interview and felt overwhelmed or helpless when you sat in the visitor's chair? Where the interviewer seemed so big and overwhelming and you felt small and insignificant? It is likely that the interviewer had cunningly arranged his office furnishings to raise his own status and power and, in so doing, to lower yours. Certain strategies using chairs and seating arrangements can create this atmosphere in an office.

The factors involved in raising status and power by using chairs are: the size of the chair and its accessories, the height of the chair from the floor and the location of the chair relative to the other person.

Chair Size and Accessories

The height of the back of the chair raises or lowers a person's status and the high-backed chair is a well-known example. The higher the back of the chair, the greater the power and status of the person sitting in it. Kings, queens, popes and other high-status people may have the back of their throne or official chair as high as 8 feet to show their status relative to their subjects; the senior executive has a high-backed leather chair and his visitor's chair has a low back.

Swivel chairs have more power and status than fixed chairs, allowing the user freedom of movement when he is placed under pressure. Fixed chairs allow little or no movement and this lack of movement is compensated by body gestures that can reveal a person's attitudes and feelings. Chairs with arm rests, those that lean back and those that have wheels are better than chairs that have not.

Chair Height

The acquisition of power using height was covered in Chapter 14 but it is worth noting that status is gained if your chair is adjusted higher off the floor than the other person's. Some advertising executives are known for sitting on high-backed chairs that are adjusted for maximum height while their visitors sit opposite, in the competitive position, on a sofa or chair that is so low that their eyes are level with the executive's desk. A common ploy is to have the ashtray just out of the visitor's reach, which forces him to be inconvenienced when ashing his cigarette.

Chair Location

As mentioned in the chapter on seating arrangements, the most power is exerted on the visitor when his chair is placed in the competitive position. A common power play is to place the visitor's chair as far away as possible from the executive's desk into the social or public territory zone, which further reduces the visitor's status.

Strategic Office Layout

Having read this book, you should now be able to arrange your office furniture in such a way as to have as much power, status or control over others as you wish. Here is a case study showing how we rearranged a person's office to help solve some of his supervisor/employee relationship problems.

John, who was an employee in an insurance company, had been promoted to a manager's position and was given an office. After a few months in the role, John found that the other employees disliked dealing with him and his relationship with them was occasionally hostile, particularly when they were in his office. He found it difficult to get them to follow his instructions and guidance and he heard that they were talking about him behind his back. Our observations of John's plight revealed that the communication breakdowns were at their worst when the employees were in his office.

For the purpose of this exercise, we will ignore management skills and concentrate on the non-verbal aspects of the problem. Here is a summary of our observations and conclusions about John's office layout:

1. The visitor's chair was placed in the competitive position in relation to John.
2. The walls of the office were timber panels except for an outside window and a clear glass partition that looked into the general office area. This glass partition reduced John's status and could increase the power of a subordinate who was sitting in the visitor's chair because the other employees were directly behind him and could see what was happening.
3. John's desk had a solid front that hid the lower part of his body and prevented the subordinates observing many of John's gestures.
4. The visitor's chair was placed so that the visitor's back was to the open door.
5. John often sat in the both-hands-behind-head position (Figure 93) and in the leg-over-chair position (Figure 129) whenever a subordinate was in his office.
6. John had a swivel chair with a high back, arm rests and wheels. The visitor's chair was a plain low-backed chair with fixed legs and no arm rests.

Considering that between 60 and 80 percent of human communication is done non-verbally, it is obvious that these aspects of John's non-verbal communication spelled disaster. To rectify the problem the following rearrangements were made:

1. John's desk was placed in front of the glass partition, making his office appear bigger and allowing him to be visible to those who entered his office.
2. The 'hot seat' was placed in the corner position, making communication more open and allowing the corner to act as a partial barrier when necessary.
3. The glass partition was sprayed with a mirror finish, allowing John to see out, but not permitting others to see in. This raised John's status and created a more intimate atmosphere within his office.
4. A round coffee table with three identical swivel chairs was placed at the other end of the office to allow informal meetings to take place on an equal level.
5. In the original layout (Figure 158), John's desk gave half the table territory to the visitor and the revised layout (Figure 159) gave John complete claim to the desk top.
6. John practiced relaxed open arms and legs gestures combined with frequent palm gestures when speaking with subordinates in his office.

The result was that supervisor/employee relationships improved and the employees began describing John as an easygoing and relaxed supervisor.

Status Raisers

Certain objects strategically placed around the office can be subtly used non-verbally to increase the status and power of the occupant. Some examples include:

1. Low sofas for visitors to sit on.
2. An expensive ashtray placed out of the reach of the visitor,

causing him inconvenience when ashing his cigarette.
3. A cigarette container from overseas.
4. Some red folders left on the desk marked 'Strictly Confidential'.
5. A wall covered with photos, awards or qualifications that the occupant has received.
6. A slim briefcase. Large, bulky briefcases are carried by those who do all the work.

All that is needed to raise your status, increase your power and effectiveness with others is a little thought given to non-verbal gymnastics in your office or home. Unfortunately, most executive offices are arranged like the one in Figure 158; rarely is consideration given to the negative non-verbal signals that are unwittingly communicated to others.

We suggest that you study your own office layout and use the preceding information to make the positive changes needed.

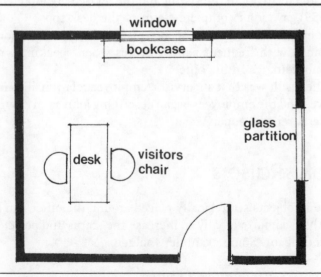

Figure 158 *Original office layout*

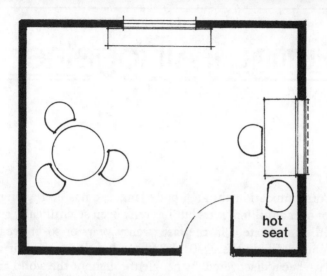

hot
seat

Figure 159   *New office layout*

Eighteen

Putting It All Together

Communication through body language has been going on for over a million years but has only been scientifically studied to any extent in the last twenty years or so; it became popular during the 1970s. By the end of this century it will have been 'discovered' by people throughout the world and I predict that its impact and meaning in human communication will be part of formal education. This book has served as an introduction to body language and I encourage you to seek further knowledge through your own research and experience and through the examples given.

Ultimately, society will be your best research and testing ground. Conscious observation of your own actions and those of others is the best way for each person to gain a better understanding of the communication methods of the earth's most complex and interesting beast—man himself.

The remainder of this book is devoted to social and business situations and shows how gestures and body signals occur in clusters and the circumstances that may affect your interpretation. However, before you read the notes, study each picture sequence and see how many you can interpret through what you have read in this book. You will be amazed to find how much your perceptiveness has improved.

Clusters, Circumstances and Gestures in Daily Encounters

Figure 160 A good example of an openness cluster. The palms are fully exposed in the submissive position and the fingers are spread wide to give more impact to the gesture. The head is in the neutral position and the arms and legs are apart. This man is communicating a submissive, non-threatening attitude.

Figure 161 This is a classic deceit cluster. As he rubs his eye he looks away towards the floor and both eyebrows are raised to the disbelief position. His head is turned away and down, showing a negative attitude. He also has an insincere, tight-lipped smile.

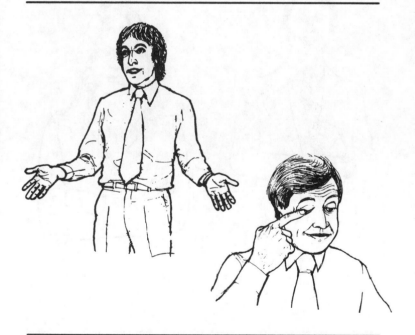

Figure 160   **Figure 161**

Figure 162 Inconsistency of gestures is obvious here. The man is smiling confidently as he crosses the room but one hand has crossed his body to play with his watch and form a partial arm barrier which shows that he is unsure of himself and/or his circumstances.

Figure 163 This woman disapproves of the person at whom she is looking. She has turned neither her head nor body toward him but is giving him a sideways glance with her head slightly down (disapproval), eyebrows slightly turned down (anger), a full arm-cross gesture (defensive) and the corners of her mouth are turned down.

Figure 162   Figure 163

Figure 164 Dominance, superiority and territoriality are evident here. Both-hands-on-head shows a superior 'know-it-all' attitude and feet-on-desk shows a territorial claim to it. To further highlight his status he has an expensive chair. He is also sitting in the competitive/defensive position.

Figure 165 The hands-on-hips gesture is used by the child to make herself appear larger and more threatening. The chin is jutting forward to show defiance and the mouth is opened wide to expose the teeth, just as animals do before they attack.

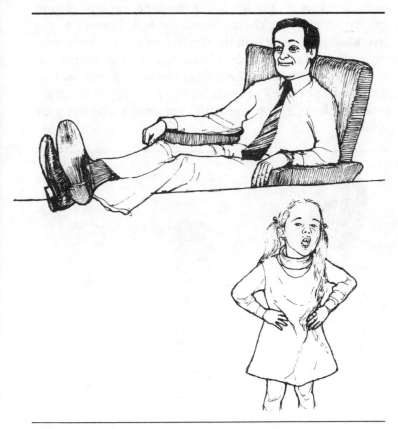

Figure 164   Figure 165

Figure 166 This cluster can be summed up in one word—negative. The folder has been used as a barrier and the arms and legs are folded due to nervousness or defensiveness. His coat is buttoned and his sunglasses hide any eye or pupil signals. Much of his face is hidden by his beard, which gives him a suspicious appearance. Considering that people form 90 percent of their opinion of someone in the first 90 seconds it is unlikely that this man will ever get to first base with another person.

Figure 167 Both men are using aggressive and readiness gestures, the man on the left using the hands-on-hips gesture and the man on the right the thumbs-in-belt. The man on the left is less aggressive than the man on the right as he is leaning backwards and his body is pointing away from the man on the right. The man on the right, however, has assumed an intimidating pose by pointing his body directly at the other man. His facial expression is also consistent with his body gestures.

Figure 166   **Figure 167**

Figure 168 The man on the left is straddling his chair in an attempt to take control of the discussion or to dominate the man on the right. He is also using the direct body point at the man on the right. He has clenched fingers and his feet are locked together under his chair, showing a frustrated attitude, which means that he is probably having difficulty in getting his point across. The man in the center feels superior to the other two because of the hands-behind-head gesture he has taken. He also has the leg-lock position, meaning that he will compete or be argumentative. He has a high-status chair that swivels, leans back and has wheels and arm rests. The man on the right is seated on a low-status chair that has fixed legs and no accessories. His arms and legs are tightly crossed (defensive) and his head is down (hostile), indicating that he does not buy what he hears.

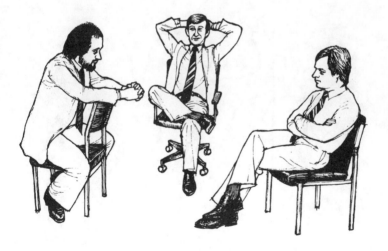

Figure 168

Figure 169 The woman is displaying the classic courtship gestures. She has one foot forward, pointing towards the man on the far left (interest), a combination of hand-on-hip and thumb-in-belt (sexual readiness), her left wrist is exposed and she is blowing cigarette smoke upwards (confident, positive). She is also giving a sideways glance to the man on the far left and he is responding to her courtship gestures by adjusting his tie (preening) and pointing his foot at her. His head is up (interested). The man in the center is obviously unimpressed with the other man as he has his body pointing away and is giving him an aggressive sideways glance. He has his palms out of sight and is blowing his cigarette smoke down (negative). He is also leaning against the wall (territorial aggression).

Figure 169

Figure 170 The man on the left is using superiority gestures and appears to have an arrogant attitude towards the man sitting opposite. He is using the eye-block signal as his brain attempts to block the other man from sight and his head is tilted back to 'look down his nose' at him. Defensiveness is also evident as his knees are held tightly together and he is holding his wine glass with both hands to form a barrier. The man in the middle has been excluded from the conversation as the other two men have not formed a triangle to include him. He does, however, seem quite aloof as shown by his thumbs-in-waistcoat gesture (superiority); he is leaning back on his chair and is using a crotch display. His head is in the neutral position. The man on the right has heard enough and has taken the starter's position (ready to leave) and his body is pointed toward the nearest exit. His eyebrows and the corners of his mouth are turned down, and his head is slightly down, all of which demonstrate disapproval.

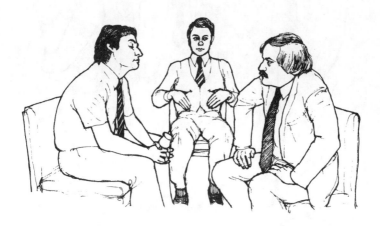

Figure 170

Figure 171 The man on the left and the man on the right have taken the closed body formation to show the middle man that he is not accepted into the conversation. The middle man's attitude shows superiority and sarcasm and he is using the lapel-grasping gesture with a thumb-up (superiority) plus a thumb-point gesture toward the man on his left (ridicule) who has responded defensively with crossed legs and aggressively with the upper-arm grip gesture (self-control) and sideways glance. The man on the left of this sequence is also unimpressed with the middle man's attitude. He has crossed legs (defensive), palm-in-pocket (unwilling to participate) and is looking at the floor while using the pain-in-neck gesture.

Figure 171

Figure 172 This sequence also shows a tense atmosphere. All three men are sitting back in their chairs to keep the maximum distance from each other. The man on the right is causing the problem because of his negative gesture cluster. As he is speaking he is using the nose-touch gesture (deceit) and his right arm has crossed his body to make a partial arm barrier (defensive). His lack of concern about the other men's opinions is shown by the leg-over-chair gesture and his body is pointed away from them. The man on the left disapproves of what the man on the right has to say as he is using the lint-picking gesture (disapproval); his legs are crossed (defensive) and pointed away (uninterested). The man in the middle would like to say something but is holding back his opinion, shown by his self-restraint gesture of gripping the arms of the chair and locked ankles. He has also issued a non-verbal challenge to the man on the right by pointing his body at him.

Figure 172

Figure 173 In this scene the man on the left and the woman have mirrored each other's gestures and are forming 'book-ends' on the couch. The couple are very interested in each other and have positioned their hands in such a way that they can expose their wrists and they have crossed their legs toward one another. The man in the middle has a tight-lipped smile which can make him appear interested in what the other man has to say but it is not consistent with his other facial and body gestures. His head is down (disapproval), his eyebrows are also down (anger) and he is giving the other man a sideways glance. In addition to this, his arms and legs are tightly crossed (defensive), all indicating that he has a very negative attitude.

Figure 173

Figure 174 The man on the left is using an excellent gesture cluster to convey openness and honesty—exposed palms, foot forward, head up, coat unbuttoned, arms and legs apart, leaning forward and smiling gestures. Unfortunately for him, however, his story is not getting across. The woman is sitting back in her chair with her legs crossed away (defensive), she has a partial arm barrier (defensive), a clenched fist (hostile), head down and is using the critical evaluation gesture (hand to face). The man in the middle is using the raised-steeple gesture, indicating that he feels confident or superior, and he is sitting in the leg-lock position, showing that his attitude is competitive or argumentative. We assume that his overall attitude is negative, as he is sitting back, his head down.

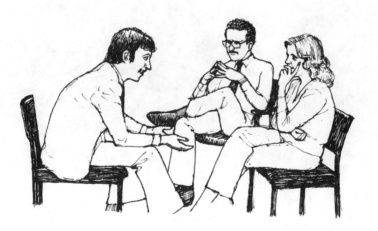

Figure 174

The following three figures show a party scene that demonstrates typical defense, aggression and courtship gesture clusters.

Figure 175 The three people all have their arms folded, two have their legs crossed (defensive) and all have their bodies oriented away from each other, all indicating that they have just met for the first time. The man on the right is very interested in the woman as he has turned his right foot around to point at her and he is giving her a sideways glance, combined with raised eyebrows (interest) and a smile; he is leaning towards her with the upper part of his body.

Figure 175

Figure 176 The non-verbal attitudes have changed. The woman has uncrossed her legs and is standing in a neutral position, while the man on the left of the sequence has uncrossed his legs and is pointing one foot at her (interest). He is using the thumbs-in-belt gesture which is intended either for the other man, in which case the attitude is one of aggression, or for the benefit of the woman, making it a sexual signal. He is also standing straighter to make himself appear bigger. The man on the right seems to have become intimidated by the other man, as seen by his more erect stance, and he is giving the man on the left a sideways glance combined with eyebrows down (disapproval) and his smile has gone.

Figure 176

Figure 177 The attitudes and emotions of those people are now clearly shown by their gestures. The man on the left has kept his thumbs-in-belt, foot-forward position and has turned his body slightly towards the woman, making it a complete courtship display. His thumbs are also gripping his belt much tighter to make the gesture more noticeable and his body has become even more erect. The woman is responding to this courtship display with her own, showing that she is interested in being involved with the man. She has uncrossed her arms, turned her body toward him and is pointing one foot at him. Her courtship gestures include hair touching, exposed wrists, chest forward with exposed cleavage and positive facial expression, and she is blowing her cigarette smoke upwards (confidence). The man on the right appears unhappy about being excluded and is using the hands-on-hips gesture (aggressive readiness) to show his displeasure.

In summary, the man on the left has won the woman's attentions and the other man should look elsewhere for a partner.

Figure 177

Bibliography

ARDREY, R., *The Territorial Imperative*, Atheneum, New York, 1966

ARGYLE, M., *The Psychology of Interpersonal Behaviour*, Penguin Books, 1967

ARGYLE, M., *Bodily Communication*, International Universities Press, New York, 1975

ARGYLE, M., *Skills with People: A Guide for Managers*, Hutchinson, London, 1973

ARGYLE, M., *Training Managers*, The Acton Society Trust, London, 1962

ARGYLE, M., *Social Interaction*, Methuen, New York, 1973

BACON, A.M., *A Manual of Gestures*, Griggs, Chicago, 1875

BELLAK, LEOPOLD, M.D., and BAKER, SAMM SINCLAIR, *Reading Faces*, Bantam Books, 1983

BENTHALL, J. and POLHEMUS, T., *The Body as a Medium of Expression*, Allen Lane, London, 1975

BERNE, E., *Games People Play*, Grove Press, New York, 1964

BIRDWHISTELL, R.L., *Introduction to Kinesics*, University of Louisville Press, Louisville, Kentucky, 1952

BIRDWHISTELL, R.L., *Kinesics and Context*, University of Pennsylvania Press, 1970

BLACKING, J., *The Anthropology of the Body*, Academic Press, London, New York, 1977

BRYAN, W.J., *The Psychology of Jury Selection*, Vantage Press, New York, 1971

BRUN, T., *The International Dictionary of Sign Language*, Wolfe Publishing, London, 1969

CALERO, H., *Winning the Negotiation*, Hawthorn Books, New York, 1979

CARNEGIE, D., *How to Win Friends and Influence People*, Simon and Schuster, New York, 1937

COLLETT, P., *Social Rules and Social Behaviour*, Rowman & Littlefield, Totowa, New Jersey, 1977

CRITCHLEY, M., *The Language of Gesture*, Folcroft Library Editions, Folcroft, Pennsylvania, 1939

CRITCHLEY, M., *Silent Language*, Butterworth, Woburn, Massachusetts, 1975

CUNDIFF, M., *Kinesics*, Parker Publishing, New York, 1972

DALE-GUTHRIE, R., *Body Hot-Spots*, Van Nostrand Reinhold, New York, 1976

DARWIN, C., *The Expression of Emotion in Man and Animals*, Appleton-Century-Crofts, New York, 1872

DAVITZ, J.R., *The Communication of Emotional Meaning*, McGraw-Hill, New York, 1964

DUNCAN, S., and FISKE, D.W., *Face-to-Face Interaction*, Erlbaum, Hillsdale, New Jersey, 1977

DUNKELL, S., *Sleep Positions*, New American Library, New York, 1978

EFFRON, D., *Gesture, Race and Culture*, Mouton, The Hague, 1972

EIBL-EIBESFELDT, I., *Ethology: The Biology of Behaviour*, Holt, Rinehart and Winston, New York, 1970

EIBL-EIBESFELDT, I., *Love and Hate: The Natural History of Behaviour Patterns*, Holt, Rinehart and Winston, New York, 1971

EKMAN, P., *Darwin and Facial Expression*, Academic Press, New York, 1973

EKMAN, P., FRIESEN, W. and ELLSWORTH, P., *Emotion in the Human Face*, Pergamon Press, New York, 1972

EKMAN, P., and FRIESEN, W., *Unmasking the Face*, Prentice-Hall, Englewood Cliffs, New Jersey, 1975

FAST, J., *Body Language*, M. Evans & Company, New York, 1970

FAST, J. and B., *Reading Between the Lines*, Viking, New York, 1979

FELDMAN, S., *Mannerisms of Speech and Gesture in Everyday Life*, International University Press, 1959

GAYLE, W., *Power Selling*, Prentice-Hall, New York, 1959

GOFFMAN, E., *Interaction Ritual*, Pantheon, New York, 1982

GOFFMAN, E., *The Presentation of Self in Everyday Life*, Doubleday, New York, 1959

GOFFMAN, E., *Behaviour in Public Places*, Free Press, Illinois, 1963

GORDON, R.L., *Interviewing Strategy, Techniques and Tactics*, Dorsey, Homewood, Illinois, 1976

HALL, E.T., *Silent Language*, Doubleday & Co., New York, 1959

HALL, E.T., *The Hidden Dimension*, Doubleday & Co., New York, 1966

HARPER, R.G., *Non-Verbal Communication; the State of the Art*, Wiley, New York, 1978

HENLEY, N.M., *Body Politics: Power, Sex and Non-Verbal Communication*, Prentice-Hall, New Jersey, 1977

HESS, E., *The Tell-Tale Eye*, Van Nostrand Reinhold, New York, 1975

HIND, R., *Non-Verbal Communication*, Cambridge University Press, London, 1972

HORE, T., *Non-Verbal Behaviour*, Australian Council for Educational Research, 1976

JAMES, W., *Principles of Psychology*, Holt, Rinehart, New York, 1892

JUNG, C., *Man and His Symbols*, Doubleday, New York, 1969

KAHN, R.I., and CANNELL, C.F., *The Dynamics of Interviewing*, Wiley, New York, 1957

KENDON, A., *Organisation of Behaviour in Face-to-Face Interaction*, Beresford Book Service, Chicago, 1975

KEY, M.R., *Non-Verbal Communication: a Research Guide and Bibliography*, Scarecrow Press, Metuchen, New Jersey, 1977

KEY, M.R., *Paralinguistics and Kinesics; Non-Verbal Communication*, Scarecrow Press, Metuchen, New Jersey, 1975

KNAPP, M., *Non-Verbal Communication in Human Interaction* (2nd edition), Holt, Rinehart and Winston, New York, 1978

KORDA, M., *Power: How To Get It, How To Use It*, Random House, New York, 1975

KORDA, M., *Power in the Office*, Weidenfeld & Nicolson, London, 1976

KORMAN, B, *Hands: The Power of Awareness*, Sunridge Press, New York, 1978

LAMB, W., *Posture and Gesture*, Duckworth, London, 1965

LAMB, W., and ELIZABETH WATSON, *Body Code*, Routledge and Kegan Paul, Boston, 1979

LEWIS, D., *The Secret Language of Your Child*, Berkley Publishing Corporation, New York, 1979

LIGGETT, J., *The Human Face*, Stein & Day, Briarcliff Manor, New York, 1974

LORENZ, K., *On Aggression*, Bantam, New York, 1970

LORENZ, K., *King Solomon's Ring*, New American Library, New York, 1967

McCROSKEY, LARSON and KNAPP, *An Introduction to Interpersonal Behaviour*, Prentice-Hall, Englewood Cliffs, New Jersey, 1971

MACHOVEC, F.J., *Body Talk*, Peter Pauper Press, New York, 1975

MALLERY, G., *The Gesture Speech of Man*, Salem, 1881

MASTERS, W.H. and JOHNSON, V.E., *Human Sexual Response*, Little, Brown, Boston, 1966

MEHRABIAN, A., *Tactics of Social Influence*, Prentice-Hall, Englewood Cliffs, New Jersey, 1969

MEHRABIAN, A., *Silent Messages*, Wadsworth, Belmont, California, 1971

MITCHELL, M.E., *How to Read the Language of the Face*, Macmillan, New York, 1968

MORRIS, D., *The Naked Ape*, McGraw-Hill, New York, 1968

MORRIS, D., *The Human Zoo*, Dell Publishing Company, New York, 1970

MORRIS, D., *Intimate Behaviour*, Cape, London, 1971

MORRIS, D., *Manwatching*, Abrams, New York, 1977

MORRIS, D., with COLLETT, MARSH and O'SHAUGHNESSY, *Gestures, their Origins and Distribution*, Stein & Day, Briarcliff Manor, New York, 1979

NIERENBERG, G., *The Art of Negotiating*, Hawthorn Books, New York, 1968

NIERENBERG, G., and CALERO, H., *How to Read a Person Like a Book*, Hawthorn Books, New York, 1971

PEASE, A.V., GARNER, A., *Talk Language—How to use Conversation for Profit and Pleasure*, Camel Publishing, Sydney 1985.

PEASE, A.V., *The Hot Button Selling System*, Elvic & Co, Sydney, 1976

PLINER, O, KRAMER, L., ALLOWAY, T., *Non-Verbal Communication*, Plenum Press, New York, 1973

REIK, T., *Listening with the Third Ear*, Farrar, Straus and Giroux, New York, 1948

SAITZ, R.L. and CERVENKA, E.C., *Handbook of Gestures: Colombia and the United States*, Mouton, Hawthorne, New York, 1972

SATHRE, F., OLSON, R., and WHITNEY, C., *Let's Talk*, Scott Foresman, Glenview, Illinois, 1973

SCHEFLEN, A.E., *Body Language and the Social Order*, Prentice-Hall, New Jersey, 1972

SCHEFLEN, A.E., *Human Territories*, Prentice-Hall, New Jersey, 1976

SCHULTZ, W.C., *A Three-Dimensional Theory of Interpersonal Behaviour*, Holt, Rinehart and Winston, New York, 1958

SIDDONS, H., *Practical Illustration of Rhetorical Gestures*, London, 1822

SOMMER, R., *Personal Space: The Behavioural Basis of Design*, Prentice-Hall, Englewood Cliffs, New Jersey, 1969

SZASZ, S., *Body Language of Children*, Norton, New York, 1978

WHITESIDE, R.L., *Face Language*, Pocket Books, New York, 1975

WHITNEY, HUBIN and MURPHY, *The New Psychology of Persuasion and Motivation in Selling*, Prentice-Hall, New Jersey, 1978

WOLFF, C., *A Psychology of Gesture*, Ayer, Salem, New York, 1972

VON CRANACH, M., *Social Communication and Movement: Studies of Interaction and Expression in Man and Chimpanzee*, Academic Press, New York, 1974